THE OFFICIAL
MANCHESTER UNITED
DIARY OF THE SEASON

THE OFFICIAL
MANCHESTER UNITED

DIARY OF THE SEASON

MANCHESTER UNITED

© Manchester United Football Club Limited 2006

The right of Manchester United Football Club Limited to be identified as the authors of this work
has been asserted by them in accordance with the
Copyright, Designs and Patents Act 1988.

First published in hardback in Great Britain in 2006 by
Orion Books
an imprint of the Orion Publishing Group Ltd
Orion House, 5 Upper St Martin's Lane,
London WC2H 9EA

1 3 5 7 9 10 8 6 4 2

A CIP catalogue record for this book is available
from the British Library.

ISBN-13: 978 0 75287 602 3
ISBN-10: 0 75287 602 3

Designed by Geoff Green Book Design, Cambridge
Printed in Great Britain by Butler & Tanner Ltd

The Orion Publishing Group's policy is to use papers that are natural, renewable and recyclable
and made from wood grown in sustainable forests. The logging and manufacturing processes are
expected to conform to the environmental regulations of the country of origin.

Every effort has been made to fulfil requirements with regard to reproducing copyright material.
The author and publisher will be glad to rectify any omissions at the earliest opportunity.

www.orionbooks.co.uk

CONTENTS

CHAPTER ONE
The takeover ... and a summer of change   1

CHAPTER TWO
Off to a perfect start   14

CHAPTER THREE
The winning stops as injuries take their toll   36

CHAPTER FOUR
Enough said: Roy Keane departs as   66
Old Trafford mourns a legend

CHAPTER FIVE
Farewell George, goodbye Europe   91

CHAPTER SIX
A cupful of woe as a domestic Double disappears   119

CHAPTER SEVEN
A Cardiff cup of joy and the toast is 'Smudger'   150

CHAPTER EIGHT
King Louis reigns but the title dream fades   168

CHAPTER NINE
Broken bones, broken hearts, but Europe here we come!   201

CHAPTER ONE

*The takeover ... and a
summer of change*

Sir Alex Ferguson summed things up perfectly.

'Manchester United is too big a carrot for someone to leave alone.'

He was looking back on the summer of 2005, a period when the club stepped into the unknown. Uncertainty hung over Old Trafford after one of the most significant events in the history of the world's best-known football club. The club had changed hands following a prolonged takeover and after fourteen years as a public limited company. So, at a time when most football fans were looking forward to the start of a new season, those who followed United had no idea what might happen.

The club had new owners, its shares having been bought up by Red Football Limited, a UK-registered company run by American businessman Malcolm Glazer and his family. No one – apart from the Glazers themselves – knew what lay ahead, but many were willing to speculate. The doom and gloom merchants saw it as the end.

In their pessimistic view, Manchester United would soon be no more. The club was destined for oblivion with the new owners running it into the ground. Star players would be sold to balance the books, with home games played against a background of empty seats. They claimed the takeover would also signal the end of the Ferguson era with Sir Alex, the most successful manager in modern-day football, and the man who had led the club to more glory than any of his predecessors, put out to graze. He would be reluctantly forced into retirement as the Americans moved in their own man.

They were wrong.

For weeks the tabloid press fanned flames of dissent with speculative stories suggesting a break-up of the United empire, and it was understandable that such conjecture caused concern among the rank and file fans. The anti-takeover lobby predicted supporters in their thousands would turn their back on the club while others would be driven away by vastly hiked ticket prices. That just did not happen.

There were protest marches, some fans spectacularly burned season ticket renewal forms in front of television cameras, giving the outside world the impression that Manchester United was a club in chaos. Meanwhile, the new owners remained silent until the takeover was completed before deciding it was time for action.

They had read the rumours, heard the whispers and noted the concern among supporters. Now they would give their side of the story and they did it through Joel Glazer, one of Malcolm's three sons drafted onto the club's re-vamped board of directors, who made a surprise appearance on MUTV. His first task was to convince doubters that the future of Manchester United – as well as that of Sir Alex Ferguson and chief executive David Gill – was in safe hands.

'Nothing will change. People will only see this with time and we can't make time move forward. We understand the scepticism; we understand that when there is change, there's uncertainty. But things are, to me, business as usual.

'David Gill will continue to do the great things he's been doing with his team. Sir Alex Ferguson will be given all the resources for him to compete on the field at the highest possible level, so we are always going to provide them with what they need, when they need it, to be successful.

'Manchester United are very fortunate, as everyone knows, to have the most wonderful manager in Sir Alex and the success he has had. He's done a tremendous job. We have the greatest respect for him and hope to work with him for many years to come.'

Joel Glazer's television appearance on 30 June, came not only as a surprise to viewers and a media eager for some crumbs from the

American camp, but to MUTV anchor man Steve Bower:

'I didn't know anything about the interview until the morning of the programme when Joel and his brothers Avram and Bryan came to the ground. The whole visit had been kept top secret but it went off without a hitch. To be quite honest, nobody quite knew what to expect. People had only heard about the Glazers and nobody had heard from them and this was the first time any of the family had spoken, so I was like everybody else and didn't know what to expect.

'I found Joel very affable, very pleasant, very approachable and during the interview he came over as being very honest as well. Certainly, everything he said has so far turned out to be true and you can only judge the new owners on their actions. So far what was said has come to fruition.

Nobody even knew they were inside Old Trafford and it was Joel who was put up for the interview. We recorded an hour special in our main studio which overlooks the Old Trafford pitch.

'It was the only interview the Glazer family did and it went all around the world, and for ages my phone never stopped. I was on CNN, TV, radio galore you name it. All these American stations ringing me asking: "Are you the guy who spoke to Joel Glazer?" It was a bit of a whirlwind twenty-four hours.'

Steve began the interview by asking why it had taken so long before letting supporters hear the Glazers' side of the story.

'That has been a little frustrating for us because people who know me and know my family, know that any time they can come up to us and approach us and we're happy to talk. Part of the problem with being a plc is you're very restricted with what you can and can't say, and when you're working under those types of guidelines everyone says you've got to be very careful. You try and say something, and if you say the wrong thing, it may have problems based on the regulations, so it was really an effort to stay clear of that.'

It was obvious he felt a return to private ownership would benefit the club.

'When you are a plc so much time and effort and energy within the organisation is spent just dealing with certain regulations, public filings, making presentations. This time could be better spent furthering the club's causes. I think people will soon realise some of the benefits to being private. But again this is a situation that takes time for people to understand.

'The thing I emphasise is this: it's going to be a long-term situation and nothing I can say today, or could have said yesterday, is going to completely change people's views. The only thing that's going to change views is things that happen over time, so I caution people that this is a marathon and not a sprint. Judge us over the long haul, don't judge us on a day or the last several months. It's very frustrating when you can't say everything you want to say. We firmly believe while there is scepticism today and uncertainty today, time will change that as well.'

Why Manchester United?

'What attracted us and allured us to Old Trafford are all the great things, all the great history, and all the great heritage. People keep saying, "What are you going to change?", and the thing I keep saying is people aren't going to notice a change. We don't want people to notice a change because in the end we'll be doing a disservice to this great club.

'We just want to help carry it on and grow what Manchester United has been, while recognising, worldwide, maybe there are some more things we can do which benefits the community and the football at large.'

Joel Glazer hoped his television appearance would quash rumours and speculation which had circulated during the takeover. He set about the task, slamming newspaper claims that iconic director Sir Bobby Charlton would be sacked, Old Trafford would be sold and leased back to pay off debts and reports the club crest would be given an Americanised facelift.

'I was talking to somebody who said they'd never seen me get so excited when this subject [Sir Bobby Charlton's sacking] came up. It's amazing what people write. If you want to talk about the fabrics or important parts of a club's history, then you could probably start with Sir Bobby. That man was a great player and he will always have an association with this club and be part of this club. He is this club in many respects, forever, and to have it any other way, well, it's disgraceful that people would even talk about it.

'We have the greatest respect for him and everything he has done not only for Manchester United but for football at large throughout the world. What an ambassador he's been for this game. We look forward to working with him for many years to come, furthering that cause.'

The leasing of Old Trafford?

'Absolutely ridiculous! That's been one of the really frustrating things we've read about and that is not going to happen. There are absolutely no plans to do that. We would have not got involved with Manchester United if we did not feel that the club, under our ownership, could continue to be the great club it has been. Our family personally has invested over £270 million.

'This great club can continue to be the great club it has been, grow even further and have no limits. That's what has brought us here. That's what's going to continue to drive this club and people should not worry about some of the crazy stuff that's been portrayed in the papers or in the media.'

And the club crest?

'People who know me, know that I'm big on tradition in any sport. I'm very averse to change. There's something beautiful about the fabric of this club. There are absolutely no plans to change that.'

He claimed he understood the passion of the fans and why some had been so sceptical about the takeover.

'Nobody likes change or uncertainty and when there's change there is uncertainty.

'We understand the fans' concerns, I understand everything that's going through their minds. It's realistic to think that way, but as time goes on and people see what this is all about … they realise things aren't changing like they thought they were going to change. The club is performing on the pitch, Rooney scores his next goal, everything is OK, and it is business as usual at Old Trafford.'

He did not try to hide his delight at being one of Manchester United's new owners.

'It's a tremendous feeling. When you're around this club, following this club, the heritage, the history when you're walking on Old Trafford, the feeling you get inside … it doesn't matter how many times you walk in, you get it every time. It's incredible. But with it comes a lot of responsibility and we take that very seriously.'

He dismissed reports Sir Alex would be forced to operate on a restricted budget in the transfer market with a ceiling of £25 million a season imposed.

'We've read about caps on transfers and again, that's just not true. We are going to provide the manager with the resources necessary to field the best team. We are there to provide the manager what he needs to compete and to win at the highest level. In this type of game you can't plan to have caps. It doesn't work. Situations arise, things change. We will not get involved with this from the start unless we can compete at the highest level, not having our hands tied. The way this club has been operating in the past is going to be the way it's going to operate in the future.

'One of the great things about this club is when they've gone into the transfer market it's been for the right reasons, not just for the sake of a headline. That will continue. The other is the history of bringing up young players through the academy. There's a connection with that kind of situation that you don't get anywhere else. It's because the player grew up with the club. That is a priority of this club and that will continue.

'There is no question that if the manager saw a player he wanted to buy he would be able to make a move for him. Nobody was more excited than us last year when the club signed Wayne Rooney. If that situation arises again, this club will be in a position to go after that player and bring him to Old Trafford, because we know players love to play here and this club will be in a position to do that absolutely.

'It's not a bottomless pit and the club has been prudent to do the right things. That is what has kept it so successful over the years; not spending unwisely, spending wisely on the right players, the right fit.

'There does have to be some restraint, but again if the manager feels it's the right situation, then you have to facilitate that. Priorities always have to start on the pitch and the focus has to be on the pitch. The priority is to do better than we did last season and better than we did the previous season. We always want to do better, always compete at the top level and I know this much – I know we have the manager to make that happen. He's been there before, he's done it before and has such a great rapport with the supporters. You take great comfort from that.'

The newly appointed director revealed that he and his family had faced sustained vilification during the takeover, hate mail, scare stories, even death threats.

'That goes with the territory and if you're not prepared for that then one should not get involved. But that's what part of the attraction is, the passion, how much people care about it and while it's frustrating to see, and I've encouraged my wife not to read the newspapers, it's what comes along with it.'

He ended his TV appearance with a message of reassurance.

'We don't like what's happened over the last several months and we are embarrassed that we have caused a lot of this to happen. We apologise for that and that we haven't been able to speak out and communicate directly, but within time people will realise that our interests are the same as their interests.

'In the end we all care. I care about the same thing the supporters care about. Things will change in the future but it takes time and I do understand that it's tough, but it's part of what comes along with this. I know what we are going to do in the future, I have confidence and faith in what I am saying, but the only way to back up words is with actions – and actions take time. I can't do everything overnight, I can't go through two seasons overnight, so things take time and I know we are very patient in a lot of things we do.

'What everyone is really here to see are the great players that this great club has, whether it's Rooney or Ronaldo or Rio Ferdinand. That's what people want to see. They don't want to hear from me.

The quicker we can get out of the way and get the focus back on the pitch, the greater everything will be.'

Manchester United's new owners had spoken.

The club was under new ownership but according to Sir Alex nothing had changed and he confidently looked forward to a twentieth year in the managerial hot seat.

'You know you are working for a great club with great history and great romance about it and a great support. Our support has got criticised because the only thing that matters to them is Man United.

'From time to time if we have a bad performance they will boo at half time or at time-up, but it is not booing as if you have been disgraced or betrayed or that over-emotional thing, they just let their feelings be known and they move on. They know, because they have been through that period of twenty-six years, a quarter of a century, without winning the league. They know what it is like to support a team in bad times, so therefore they will stand by us and trust us to get the job done properly.'

The manager had already made his first ventures in the transfer market under the new regime, two weeks before Joel Glazer faced the TV cameras.

With goalkeeper Roy Carroll's offer of a new contract withdrawn shortly after United lost the FA Cup final to Arsenal and Tim Howard still finding his feet in the Premiership, the manager made a move for a new 'keeper. Terms were agreed with Fulham for Holland international Edwin van der Sar, who finally arrived at Old Trafford after being linked with United in 1999 when he was with Ajax.

'I am delighted to have signed for Manchester United, one of the most famous clubs in the world. I'm looking forward to joining my new team-mates to start preparations for the new season, which promises to be one of the most exciting of my career.'

Sir Alex was equally happy to land his man.

'Edwin brings a wealth of experience to the team. He is an international goalkeeper with proven class.'

There was plenty of other transfer speculation with Manchester

United said to be chasing three Michaels, Essien of Lyon, Ballack of Bayern Munich and England star Owen of Real Madrid, but no move materialised.

The one other major close season signing saw South Korean international Ji-sung Park move for £4 million from PSV Eindhoven, breaking new ground as he became the first of his countrymen to pull on a United shirt.

Ji-sung was confident he would cope.

'I understand the pressure of coming to Manchester United and the expectations of the fans over here, I also know that many Koreans see Manchester United as the best in the world and there will be a lot of focus on me. But I can handle that. I think I will be OK. I have no worries about it. I can overcome all that pressure and believe I will be able to perform as I expect.'

The signings were hardly bank-breaking transfer deals, but Sir Alex noticed one major change, and put this down to the club's return to private ownership.

'There was a difference straight away when it came to things like buying a player. Under the plc I would speak to Martin Edwards as the chief executive and he would have his own views, and he would then put it to the plc board. That was the structure, and when Peter Kenyon took over it was exactly the same, then David Gill. First them, then the board.

'There was always a financial awareness. Anything you did you had to notify the City and while I wouldn't say it was a handicap or anything like that, it just meant it was alerting people. Other people would know if you were after somebody. You could lose him at the last minute because of that, if you think about it.'

The United boss is a firm believer that the fewer people who know his business, the better. Even when it comes to declaring his line-up ahead of a game, Sir Alex will wait until the last minute to avoid the opposition knowing his plans. By removing those working in the City from the equation, he eradicated one possible source of a leak.

'To be honest, I was never convinced about the plc to begin with.

I am still not convinced it was the right thing to do, but in fairness, I think what helped us was the success of the team. It helped us through that phase, so the support was focussed on the team's performances and it glossed over the fact it was a major shift for Manchester United to go public.

'In the end you just settled into it and developed. And of course we had Sir Roland Smith [the late first chairman of the plc], and a man of his experience was vital to it. He was marvellous and probably he, more than anyone, eased all the change. He made it easy for everyone and he was comfortable with people, and he was really a tremendous leader of people. You felt comfortable with Roland, so if you felt that way you were able to go and do your job with confidence.

'The takeover in the summer was one of those situations which came about because the minute we went plc, you were always aware that somebody was going to buy it. Manchester United is too big a carrot for someone to leave alone. I always felt that a private owner would come in somewhere along the line, because there is so much wealth in the world today that you could say to yourself "there is somebody who will think so much of Man United they will want to buy it", but I was quite comfortable with that.'

It was not the first time an attempt had been made to buy the club during Ferguson's two decades in charge, or for the manager to find himself pondering his future. In August 1989, businessman Michael Knighton struck a deal with the then chairman Martin Edwards, but complications saw that takeover called off and led to United following the road to public flotation. During its early days, when it looked as though Knighton would succeed, doubts were also cast about the manager's future.

'At that time I remember saying to myself, "What the hell's going on?" You just didn't know. You don't know your new owners, therefore all you did was read all the negative press about the Glazers and there was a lot of that.

'Then you had that negative issue about the independent supporters. [IMUSA – the Independent Manchester United Supporters'

Association – had opposed the takeover, joining forces with Shareholders United, the body formed by the banding together of some of the club's small investors.] I had them phoning my house and things like that, telling me to resign but they seemed to forget that I have brought at least ... well, I've brought everybody here!

'The likes of Les Kershaw has been with me eighteen years, Dave Bushell, Jim Ryan, Tony Whelan, Paul McGuinness, Mike Phelan, Brian McClair they have been here with me virtually from the beginning, or at least over ten or twelve years and I said, "What happens to my staff if I go?" I feel that I have a responsibility to them. Need them to stay in a job, not me. So, therefore, there was a lot of hot air and a lot of unfair criticism because nobody actually knew the people.

'To make judgements on people you don't know? I can understand people thinking they have got to protect the club, and I am fully aware of that, but all these protests should have been done when they went plc. That was the time to protest because thereafter Manchester United was never going to be the same.'

A year on and the manager maintained his stance that, as far as he was concerned, life on Old Trafford's transfer front had improved.

'In the main the Glazers have been far more flexible and easier to deal with than the plc in that respect because so far anything I have asked for they have said fine. I can only judge people on how I deal with them, and they have been terrific. It is terrific even from David Gill's point of view because he has far more freedom and flexibility to run the football club. He has phone meetings with them and that sort of thing, and it is just a matter of carrying on.

'For me it is exactly the same. They have never interfered in any shape or form with anything. They have been great. They have just let us get on with it because they know we can manage. They know David Gill can manage, he is an outstanding chief executive. They know it works and they are just letting us get on with it.

'I am more than happy with the way things have gone and they have respected our position very well. The brothers have come over from time to time and they are getting used to Man United. You can read all the history books in the world about our club but once you get in here – and I experienced this when I came down here – you sort of get woven into the fabric of the place and therefore you become almost a fan yourself.'

There were those who disagreed. Some who had followed the club before it changed hands decided they could no longer support Manchester United. Members of those groups which had actively opposed the takeover decided it was time to quit a ship they felt was heading for the rocks. They formed their own football team, a venture which attracted plenty of publicity but an act which did not go down well with Sir Alex, in whose eyes loyal supporters stand by their club no matter what.

'I'm sorry about that. It is a bit sad that part, but I wonder just how big a United supporter they are. They seem to me to be promoting or projecting themselves a wee bit, rather than saying at the end of the day that the club has made a decision, "we'll stick by them". It is more about them than us.

'From the day I came here, Martin Edwards more than anyone experienced the vent of a lot of the fans. His whole family did. I am not going into that because I don't know the reasons, because I wasn't here during that period when Louis Edwards took over or anything like that, but for some reason Martin was never the flavour of the month, the blue-eyed boy with them. They started talking about director representation from the supporters then there was IMUSA and Shareholders United at the time of the BSkyB bid and they got a platform.'

Satellite television company British Sky Broadcasting came close to taking over United seven years before the Glazers arrived on the scene. Eventually the deal was called off as the Monopolies Commission intervened, ruling there might be complications should a major television company own a leading football club.

'I was totally against the deal because I didn't think it was right,' says Sir Alex, 'but they feel they were responsible for stopping the BSkyB deal, which is not true. Absolutely not true. They may have made their voice heard but they were not responsible, it was the

Monopolies Commission which stopped that. Because of that it has carried on to the degree where they actually think they have got a say in the running of the football club. That is the reason why a lot of them have quit.'

Life would go on at Old Trafford, and for Sir Alex and his players it was time to get down to work.

CHAPTER TWO

Off to a perfect start

The pre-season training camp at Vale do Lobo could not have been in more idyllic surroundings. Palm trees swayed gently in the breeze above a stretch of golden Algarve sand, lush lawns threaded past plush accommodation, but as one member of the party (who prefers to remain anonymous!) put it: 'As far as torture chambers go, it was one of the nicest I've ever been in!'

Pre-season is a time footballers love to hate. It is like everyone's Monday morning; a sign that summer is ending and another campaign about to start. Vale do Lobo meant hard work, and plenty of it, but this time there was a twist thrown in: a pre-season perk for the players and their families. Keen to start at a higher level of fitness than previous years, the manager opted for a new approach. Training would commence earlier than usual, which meant cutting short the players' summer break, but he also swapped dubious English weather and sessions at the club's Trafford Training Centre at Carrington on the outskirts of Manchester, for fitness-finding in the Portuguese sunshine.

To make up for any holiday disruption, Sir Alex told the players to invite their families along too, and that was a move Ryan Giggs fully endorsed.

'It was great and I reckon it was a real success. We enjoyed ourselves, got fit and spent a bit of time with our families as well. It was something new, something I had never done before, but I certainly think it was a success. I took my girlfriend and my little girl along, and it was great seeing all the families getting together and all the kids playing. In the morning we did our training, then in the after-noon we just went out and enjoyed ourselves.

'It was no boot camp, but it was training every morning – do all your stuff, then the rest of the day you were free. The spirit was great because of it. It was also good for the new players and those who weren't too familiar with the other families; it was a great way for them all to get to know one another. There is always a good team spirit with United, but this made it even better.'

The previous season started badly, which was why Sir Alex had a re-think. This time round, he wanted to hit the ground running. With Rio Ferdinand part way through an eight-month suspension for missing a random drugs test, Cristiano Ronaldo and new signing Gabriel Heinze taking a break after Olympic duty in Greece, Ruud van Nistelrooy, Louis Saha, Wes Brown and new signing Wayne Rooney all injured, the manager was forced to field a patched-up side for the opening game of 2004–05 at Stamford Bridge. United lost 1–0 and, according to Sir Alex, that was that.

'We were playing catch-up from that moment and we never caught them. We say we lost the league in the first game and that changed our preparation and approach. This time, from day one, we hope to be up and running. That is why we came in early for pre-season training. We had to do that in relation to our trip to China and being in the qualifying round of the Champions League, but we wanted to be ready to start the season flying, fitness guaranteed.

'We have always worked on the principle that we can build up as the season goes along, but it isn't looking like that now. It is looking like a very competitive, must-win-right-away season. This is a hard league – the hardest league in the world. Winning it is itself very dif-ficult. Chelsea have raised the bar and made us take notice, but that makes me more determined and we want to win it this time.'

That determination resulted in the working break in Portugal, where any extra ounces acquired during the summer would swiftly be sweated off.

'Because there were no major international interruptions, the players reported back on 27 June, and we went to Portugal for a week. It was fantastic. Everybody loved it. We took the families with us. They all had their own houses, some of them brought their families, some brought nannies, cousins, some brought friends and we were free with that. It was up to them who they brought along.

'We hired a charter flight and I felt it was a great start. In the morning we would breakfast at a quarter to nine, then would go for a little jog and all the training ground would be laid out. It was magnificent. They had it perfect. We had a weights room in the open air with a canopy over it so it was nice and cool, and in all honesty you could not have got better preparation.'

The seven-day camp gave the new players an opportunity to mix with their team-mates and one of the first to impress was South Korean Ji-sung Park.

'He never stopped running or smiling. No matter how hot it was. I don't know where he got his energy from. I think he is going to surprise a few defenders this season. He's a very tricky and nippy player with two good feet and I reckon he'll cause teams lots of problems,' was John O'Shea's assessment.

However, if one Irishman was enjoying life in Portugal, back home fans were led to believe that another had not. Newspaper reports claimed Roy Keane and Sir Alex had been involved in an argument over the decision to allow ancillaries on the trip.

Between the summer camp and the club tour to the Far East, the manager was back behind his desk with other business to complete. Both Rio Ferdinand and Cristiano Ronaldo had been offered new contracts, but with the start of the season approaching, neither had put pen to paper. When news leaked out, it sparked speculation that Ferdinand was heading for Chelsea and that Ronaldo was ready to join his Brazilian namesake at Real Madrid.

Sir Alex rubbished the reports as best he could, also denying rumours that Ruud van Nistelrooy was leaving, that Louis Saha was rejoining Fulham, that Everton were chasing Paul Scholes, that John O'Shea was destined for Newcastle and that

Alan Smith was a target of Rangers.

Ronaldo's contract talks were delayed largely because his representative was based in Portugal and also because his father was seriously ill. The player handed the coveted No. 7 shirt after signing from Sporting Lisbon in 2003, made it clear that he wanted to remain at Old Trafford.

'We have spoken about the important questions and I believe that I will sign with Manchester United, but still I have not signed the contract to date. The negotiations are going well. My agent Jorge Mendes is responsible for this and I expect a happy solution. I am happy to sign, but I have two more years on my contract. The proposition is for another three years. I am settled at Manchester United, but if the club decides my exit, there is nothing I can do. It is the decision of the coach, but I am happy at United. No one knows the future, but I intend to fulfil my contract. I reiterate that I am calm about my future.'

Calmness was perhaps not the perfect description of the approach taken by some fans, who took the delay in Rio Ferdinand signing as an indication that he was on his way. He became the target of criticism from his own fans at friendly games in Antwerp, Clyde and Peterborough, but stuck to his guns. He would sign when he was ready, even after Sir Alex made it clear he wanted things sorted out quickly.

'It has created speculation and an unnecessary agenda for the club we don't want. Rio has received a fantastic offer. We want to be ready for the Champions League qualifier next month with everyone currently at the club remaining here. That can be solidified by Rio signing his contract and I hope he does.'

That Champions League qualifier was an unwanted curtain raiser to the Premiership season. It was on the fixture list as a reminder that United had failed to make the runner-up spot three months earlier, which would have given them automatic entry into the competition's group phase. Finishing third meant they were faced with a two-legged knock-out tie against as-yet-unknown opposition to reach that stage.

The Far East tour was underway before the draw was made, but there were more pressing issues for Sir Alex once in Hong Kong: Roy Keane was left at home and the media wanted to know why.

Some sources claimed Keane was missing following that row in Portugal, that he had been left behind as a punishment. In fact, he had stayed at Carrington to continue treatment on an injury, but once again Sir Alex found himself forced to deal with the rumour-mongers. This time he was helped by Keane's legal adviser, Michael Kennedy, who issued a statement insisting the claims were 'without foundation', but the manager's route was more direct.

Asked where his captain was at the press conference ahead of the opening tour game in Hong Kong, he responded with a curt, but to the point: 'Roy Keane is injured. It is as simple as that. You can't travel if you are injured. There is nothing else to say.'

Also missing were Cristiano Ronaldo, Wes Brown and Gabriel Heinze. Ronaldo would join the tour a few days later after spending more time with his father; Heinze was taking his summer break after international duty; while Brown was back in the treatment room.

'I was feeling my Achilles and we thought it was better to get that sorted out. I could probably have played on, but we felt it was better to get it sorted out and be back, say October time, being fit and ready to go. It happened when we were at the camp in Portugal. I had a little bit of a problem the previous season when I felt a twinge. You can play on with it, but eventually it does get very bad and you have to stop and we didn't want it to get to that point, so we decided to get it sorted and we made sure I was flying before I even tried to get a game.

'In the past, I have come back and gone straight into the team, but this time I would have a good few weeks' training first,' said the unlucky central defender.

The tour opened with an impressive win 2–0 win in Hong Kong where Giuseppe Rossi and Dong Fangzhou scored ... Dong Fangz-who? The Chinese striker is currently playing for United's Belgian feeder club Royal Antwerp and is eventually expected to find his way to Old Trafford.

Events then switched to mainland China, where Beijing Hyundai were beaten 3–0. Paul Scholes scored twice with Ji-sung Park adding the other. Then it was off to Japan where Tokyo side Kashima Antlers shook the Reds almost as much as a first-half earthquake, by winning 2–1.

However, it was television pictures of an apparent row between Ruud van Nistelrooy and Rio Ferdinand as they left the pitch that caused tremors back home. It fired off more speculation about Ferdinand's future and the story was still simmering when the tour ended in Saitama on 30 July, and J-League side Urawa Red Diamonds were beaten 2–0.

This time it was Wayne Rooney's turn to get among the goals and his double hit left him a happy man. Not so, Louis Saha. Just when everything seemed to be going so well for the unlucky Frenchman, the injury jinx that had hampered his progress at Old Trafford struck again.

'I was flying at the pre-season camp. I was feeling great. I had done my detoxification, tried to lose weight and made sure every-thing was fine. I did all the runs they asked me to do, but it is only when you come to games you can see how fit you are, so I was very, very happy. Then life decided it would be hard on me. That's life!

'In pre-season, I think you are in a kind of a fragile state and I started to feel my knee when it was hot in China. Something hap-pened. It was bad luck on me again and I don't wish that on anyone because I think I have had my share. It was very hard to take and why I think it was harder than before was because I had done the whole pre-season feeling fine and without injury. I was so motivated to do something because it was a great opportunity to respond to the critics and when something like this happens you don't understand why.'

Saha had been troubled by knee problems picked up on inter-national duty since the early days of his United career. Injury forced him to miss most of the 2004–05 season and now he was faced with another spell on the sidelines before the new term had even started. Immediately the tour ended and the party returned to England,

Louis saw a specialist and was booked in for a knee operation.

'I wasn't worried about the surgery because at the start it was only supposed to be two weeks out. I thought, "Oh that's nothing," but when you wake up and they give you crutches to walk with and say to you "It's going to be three months" that was the hardest thing I have felt in my life. It was too much to cope with and that is why, when I was able to start training again, I was happy to work for three or four hours in a row. I suppose things like this make me stronger. It was August and the season had not even started, but when it did, I knew I was going to miss the first three months!'

The rest of the squad continued the build-up for the first game.

United had been drawn against Hungarian champions Debreceni VSC in the Champions League qualifier with the first leg at Old Trafford on Tuesday 9 August, but five days before the game the squad lost another of its members – this time permanently, as Phil Neville reached a major crossroads in his career. He wanted regular first-team football, but had been unable to establish a permanent place in the side after breaking through from the lower ranks in 1996.

He was faced with a difficult decision and for elder brother Gary it was an equally trying time: 'Through the summer speaking to Phil, it came to the point where he thought he would probably have to try a new challenge. But you are always weighing things up and telling yourself, "Once I leave that's it. I won't be coming back." It's a massive decision for any lad who has come through the ranks and who only knows this club to have to say it's probably time to leave.

'During pre-season there were rumours circulating, then one night I said to Philip that he should go and speak to the manager. We went round to his house and talked it through with him. The manager said he didn't have any great desire to let Phil go, and at that point nobody had met his valuation or made any offers. He told us that if anybody made an offer he would make Phil aware of it and he was as honest as ever.'

Gary had already adjusted to life without best friend David Beckham and other close friends like Nicky Butt and Ben Thornley.

Now he was about to lose another team-mate; one who was even closer to him than the others.

'It is a huge wrench for me to see lads like Becks and Butty leave, because you have grown through so much with them. You want it to last forever, but you are realistic enough to know as a football player that it can't. Times do move on.'

Phil Neville's transfer request was equally tough for Sir Alex to take.

'We had a long chat. Phil was probably one of my favourite players. His whole family is so orientated to Manchester United and so devoted to the club that you have to give them their complete consideration rather than the club's. The boy was hurting because he wasn't getting a regular game and, with the World Cup coming up in the summer, I didn't want him destroyed in that way. When they came out to my house we decided to conduct things the best possible way to get him a top club, a good club, and to do our best to make sure it was done the right way. I think we did that.'

On Thursday 4 August, nine days before United's Premiership campaign would start with an away game at Goodison Park, Philip Neville signed for Everton. He chose his words well when asked how it felt to leave the club of his dreams: 'David Moyes was the first manager to show an interest, and the first one that I met. I have always gone along with the thought that if somebody desperately wants you, then you have got to meet them face to face. As soon as I met him there was no other club that I was going to sign for.

'Everything he said in terms of his plans for the next five years was all that I hoped for. The move also means that I can stay in the North West. I have a great contract, I'm joining a great club with great traditions and a set of players with tremendous team spirit and that is something I have always been used to.

'Leaving United is the hardest decision I have ever had to make. I had been there for eighteen years and I have obviously got strong connections and strong feelings for that club, but it got to the stage where, for my career, I had to move on and for the next five years of my contract I hope to show the same commitment to Everton that I showed to United.'

He left with a glowing testimony from his former manager: 'Phil was a fantastic servant to Manchester United and to me, and he will always be welcome here. He is probably somebody who will come back to the club at some point.'

No sooner was that deal done than Rio Ferdinand secured his future. On the eve of the Debreceni game, Sir Alex opened his press conference by announcing that the England central defender had accepted terms for a new four-year deal.

'We have made our point about Rio. We have addressed it in the proper way. His training has been terrific. He has given one hundred per cent on the football field and that is all we should concern ourselves with. Rio is a Manchester United player, he is pulling that strip on and I expect the fans to get behind him.'

It was Sir Alex's way of telling those who had jeered Ferdinand that they were wrong. The player himself had more to say on the subject.

'It's not nice when you are getting stick from some supporters, particularly over something that was never true. I will never forget how the club stood by me during my eight-month ban last year and, of course, it hurts to suggest I would throw that loyalty back in their face. I have got a thick skin and have always accepted that criticism is something that comes with the territory. You are up there to be shot at when you play for a club like Manchester United and it's up to you to deal with it. But the supporters were reading all sorts of stuff about me that was totally wide of the mark and that has made things difficult in recent weeks.'

He bared his soul in an exclusive interview with a tabloid newspaper denying suggestions that he had turned down the club's offer of £100,000 a week and demanded £120,000 a week.

'I don't know where those stories came from, but it was a load of rubbish. I can't blame the fans for wondering what was going on. I would have asked the same questions if I was reading some of that stuff. Other United players were naturally asking me about developments, but I told them I would be staying at United and that was always my intention. I will be signing a new contract this week. The deal runs until 2009, but hopefully I can stay on beyond that,' he said.

The following evening a shirt-sleeved crowd poured into Old Trafford ready to see United step into the unknown. Few knew what to expect from Debreceni, but there was a buzz of excitement in the air because football was about to re-start after an eventful close season. It was pretty lively in the press box, too.

Sir Alex's welcoming message in the match programme was pure 'Fergie hits back!' The manager wanted to end the speculation that had haunted him for weeks and felt that the printed word was the best way of doing it.

'I would have preferred to have started by striking a positive note and discussing the challenge that lies ahead of us, but I must first clear up one or two of the stories that dogged us on our Far East tour and clouded our pre-season preparations,' he wrote.

'We had hardly flown out before Rio Ferdinand's contract was hitting the headlines. It's annoying, but that's the media for you. I feel very uncomfortable when I see a guy in a United shirt being booed. It's not the true spirit of the club. The press also jumped upon an argument between Rio and Ruud, triggered by an attempted piece of play between the two players that broke down. Rio probably felt Ruud hadn't made enough effort to move away from his marker in order to receive the ball; Ruud on the other hand perhaps felt Rio had been too slow to give him the ball. Either way, it was one of those things that happen all the time in games and training, only this time it came near the end of a defeat against Kashima Antlers in Tokyo. Tempers were probably frayed at that time, so it looked worse than it was.

'In my book, there is nothing wrong in players feeling passionate about performances and results, even if it does end up as an argument. I would much rather have that, than two players walking off with one of them saying with a laugh, "Oh thanks for your pass that could have got my leg broken" and the other guy saying, "Oh, any time!" I wish I had even more of that kind of passion and commitment in the team. I do want players to care, but of course the press overplays this kind of thing. It was an argument, for heaven's sake, nothing more, nothing less.

'Then there was another argument blown up out of all proportion. Roy Keane and I had a few words at our training camp in Portugal, but as I say, an argument is nothing. Did he walk out? Did we come to blows? Of course not. We are both combustible characters and we are always having arguments. I wish I had a pound for every row I have had with Roy. You see, he cares and I care, and every so often we clash in pursuit of our ambition. That doesn't affect the respect I have for him and I don't think it lessens my standing as the manager in Roy's eyes.

'I feel slightly stupid having to explain the background to all these petty disputes, but the media makes so much of them that I can't let them go unchallenged. The press have their own agenda with their own interests at heart, not Manchester United's, and we must not let them undermine our solidarity and spirit.'

With that off his chest, Sir Alex took his seat as United stepped out to face Debreceni. They were no Real Madrid or AC Milan, but he treated them with respect, fielding his strongest available side.

TUESDAY 9 AUGUST 2005

SCORERS:
Rooney 7,
Van Nistelrooy 49,
Ronaldo 63

ATTENDANCE:
51,701

UEFA Champions League, Third Qualifying Round (first leg)
Manchester United 3   Debreceni 0

UNITED: VAN DER SAR, NEVILLE, FERDINAND, SILVESTRE, O'SHEA, FLETCHER, KEANE (SMITH 68), SCHOLES, ROONEY, VAN NISTELROOY (ROSSI 82), RONALDO (PARK 68).
SUBS NOT USED: HOWARD, HEINZE, MILLER, RICHARDSON.

Seven minutes gone and watched from the directors' box by the Glazer brothers, Wayne Rooney opened his account, smashing home a loose ball after his bid to lay a goal on for van Nistelrooy failed. Rooney's pass was half cleared, but the ball fell back to him and he struck with a low right-foot shot.

Four minutes into the second half and van Nistelrooy did get on the scoresheet, with Rooney the catalyst, setting up his striking partner with an inch-perfect final pass, which the eager Dutchman forced home.

It was the perfect start and it was only a matter of time before the third goal came. When it did, it was the third member of the 3Rs who scored it, as Cristiano Ronaldo put the result beyond doubt by finishing off a fine sixty-third minute move, which also involved Rooney and Ruud.

Sir Alex was satisfied: 'I would have settled for a 3-0 scoreline before the kick-off, in fact I would do that in any European game. The great benefit is we haven't lost a goal and we can go there in a comfortable position, but not complacent, and we have a good opportunity to advance to the group section. The front three all looked sharp and it was good that they all scored. They are all capable of having good goal-scoring seasons and if that is the case, it gives us a tremendous opportunity to do something big this year.'

The challenge of the Premiership was four days away and things were also looking good on the injury front.

'We have got only one player missing and that is Louis Saha. In that context, we always want to get to the first game of the season with everyone fit. If you have just one missing then that really is a bonus. They are all back playing: Gabi Heinze has had his three weeks' break after the Confederations Cup, Quinton Fortune is back in training and so is Wes Brown, so fingers crossed we will keep the majority of them fit for the next few weeks.'

The new season would begin with an early kick-off at Everton, but before that there was more contract talk from the manager. Paul Scholes had signed a new four-year deal and Sir Alex backed up his earlier announcement that Ferdinand had agreed terms, but confirming that everything was now settled. The defender had put pen to paper and no one was more relieved than Rio himself: 'To be honest I just wanted to get it all done and dusted. It seemed to take ages to sort out. Both the club and I were negotiating, but these things can take time. It took about four months from when we first started and I don't think that's a long time by anybody's reckoning compared to what it has taken to negotiate some contracts before that – and since. Mine went considerably quicker than most, but because the situation got highlighted, people started jumping on the bandwagon.

'At no time did I ever say I wanted to leave. Right from the beginning I said I was going to sign and I wanted to stay and I kept true to my word. But when the fans turn against you, it's hard to take. That's when you have to call upon your own inner strength, your own determination and your thick skin!

'I pulled on all those resources and got through. I just continued to play my football and that is all I could do at the time. It was great it was sorted out right at the start of the season. From the beginning I said that me coming out saying, "I'm going to sign, I'm going to sign" week in, week out would have been no good to anybody. Until I signed there would still be question marks. I just waited until I had signed and all the question marks disappeared straightaway.'

Sir Alex endorsed Ferdinand's comments.

'It's absolutely brilliant to get it done and dusted. There was a lot of nonsense in the papers about his demands that was a million miles away from what we were negotiating, but that's the way the world is now. We're delighted he's signed, with Darren Fletcher and John O'Shea also signing and Cristiano Ronaldo signing next week, it means we have a team that can stay together for four years now and that is fantastic news.'

Next stop Goodison Park.

SATURDAY 13 AUGUST 2005

Barclays Premiership
Everton 0   Manchester United 2

UNITED: VAN DER SAR, NEVILLE, FERDINAND, SILVESTRE, O'SHEA, FLETCHER (HEINZE 72), KEANE, SCHOLES (SMITH 81), PARK (RICHARDSON 85), ROONEY, VAN NISTELROOY. SUBS NOT USED: HOWARD, ROSSI.

SCORERS:
Van Nistelrooy 44, Rooney 46

ATTENDANCE: 38,610

It's only fate that the first league game should be against United and for me it is the best-case scenario,' said Phil Neville before pulling on the blue of Everton. 'Let's get the game out of the way quickly.

'In terms of the start of the season for Everton, it's a tough one. No team likes coming to Goodison and I know that from an opposition player's point of view, but we have to make sure the bigger picture is about Everton beating United and nothing about Philip Neville.

'While it was strange leaving United, it will be even stranger to be playing in a team for the first time in my career without my brother being there, but it's something I have got to live with. I have to make new friends here at Everton. Obviously my brother is there for life.'

Big brother Gary was there wearing the red of United, but if it was a big day for the Nevilles, it was even bigger for Wayne Rooney.

Cries of 'Once a Blue always a Manc!' rang from the banks of home supporters as the former favourite of every Evertonian trotted out for his third visit to Goodison since joining United. He echoed Phil Neville's thoughts.

'I suppose it had to be the opening game, but I was actually quite pleased because if it had been halfway through the season you would be thinking about it coming up. To get it over and out of the way early on was good for me. To get the win and actually score was brilliant,' said Wayne.

The Rooney goal came in the first minute of the second half, giving United a 2–0 lead after Ruud van Nistelrooy had scored in the last minute of the first.

'My goal was a bit of a gift. Joseph Yobo rolled the ball into my path and I couldn't really miss, but it was great to score there because I do get a bit of unfair stick when I go back. That's football though. Football fans are like that and it happens. It is part and parcel of the game, but it's nothing to me,' he added.

United were up and running, with Wayne Rooney happy to declare he is enjoying life at the other end of the Manchester Ship Canal.

'I'm sure if you ask anybody about the club they'll tell you that my heart is fully with Manchester United. I want to play here for years and years to come, so I have no hard feelings and no regrets about leaving Everton. Since coming to United I've learned something about the history of this club and about the players who have played here and the trophies the club has won.

'Through the nineties and early 2000s when I was watching football and trying to become a football player, Man United were ruling England and once I knew they were interested in me there was only one place I was coming.'

Rooney's move in August 2004 had stunned Evertonians, but had Sir Alex got his way, Wayne would have joined United even earlier. The manager monitored Rooney's progress after learning of the potential of the Liverpool schoolboy.

'Yes. He's told me that now, but it would have been difficult to leave Everton when I was fourteen. At that time you just want to try and play football and that's it. You don't think about anything else.'

With the first game over, Gary Neville was also able to look back on what had been an unusual afternoon.

'I didn't really feel much of it at first, then I got out on the pitch and it was strange at first seeing Phil there in another shirt. I suppose I'll get used to it over a period of time, but we were thankful to have won the game.

'Phil nearly scored. I suppose that would have been the perfect day for everybody concerned if we had won 2–1 and he had scored the goal. Perhaps not for Phil because he wanted to win the game, but everybody wishes him all the best.'

The 2006 World Cup was less than a year away and the first week of the new season was interrupted by midweek international friend-lies, but Sir Alex withdrew Gary from the England squad so that he could continue having treatment on a groin problem. It was when he returned to Carrington that the stark realisation brother Phil was no longer around hit home.

'After thirteen years of coming into training every day and seeing your brother, you just sort of get used to it. Before that it was school every day and apart from a year or so when he was still at school and I had joined United, we had been together. Not seeing each other every day was unusual, but that's life.

'We knew it would come one day and we had been so lucky for so long playing in the same team. I'll miss him as well as I miss the lads who have left like Chris Casper and Ben Thornley. Lads who I grew up with. When they leave you miss them because you create a special bond with them. We went through a lot together, growing up in the Youth Team and in the Centre of Excellence.'

By the end of the week those players who had been on inter-national duty had returned, and the manager was able to finalise his plans for the home game against Aston Villa.

'Everybody has come back fit from the internationals and that's a bonus. Wes Brown and Ryan Giggs are back training and they'll be available for next Wednesday's game in Hungary,' Sir Alex announced before kick-off.

The season was in its infancy, but the game was crucial.

Rivals Chelsea and Arsenal were due to clash at Stamford Bridge the following day and this was United's chance to get ahead of one – or both of them.

'It is strangely early for a top-of-the-table clash in the second match of the season, but we did play Chelsea in the first game of the season last year. The most important thing for us is to do our job properly and I don't really care what happens on Sunday. I just want us to get three points,' added the manager.

SATURDAY 20 AUGUST 2005

SCORER:
Van Nistelrooy 66
ATTENDANCE:
67,934

Barclays Premiership

Manchester United 1   Aston Villa 0

UNITED: VAN DER SAR, NEVILLE, FERDINAND, SILVESTRE, O'SHEA (HEINZE 59),

FLETCHER, KEANE, SCHOLES, PARK (RONALDO 59), ROONEY (SMITH 78),

VAN NISTELROOY. SUBS NOT USED: HOWARD, RICHARDSON.

Sir Alex stuck to the starting line-up used at Goodison Park, but United had to work hard to beat a Villa side that defended doggedly as David O'Leary desperately tried to end a run of fourteen managerial visits to Old Trafford without a win.

Goalless after an hour, Sir Alex made adjustments.

Cristiano Ronaldo and Gabriel Heinze replaced Ji-sung Park and John O'Shea, and within minutes both came close to scoring, thwarted only by some brilliant keeping from Thomas Sorensen. Then came the break the Reds wanted.

In the sixty-sixth minute Ronaldo crossed, Villa defender Olof Mellberg tried to head clear, but could only deflect the ball to Ruud van Nistelrooy and the alert Dutchman tapped home inside the six yard box.

Two games played, two games won.

'There are goals here – I can smell them!' claimed a smiling Sir Alex.

He also scented trouble. Next up was the trip to Hungary for the return leg against Debreceni and, from past experience, he was not too happy about having the game switched to the national stadium in Budapest.

'The pitch in Budapest is not a good pitch. We played there a couple of years ago and, while it is a big pitch, it's not even, in fact I think it's pretty ragged.'

Before United flew out he made it clear that he would be switching things around in his starting line-up: 'I'm not going to make wholesale changes, but Ryan Giggs and Wes Brown trained on Saturday morning with a view to giving them a spell. Those two definitely need a bit of football and Alan Smith is another one. Hopefully we will also be able to bring on Kieran Richardson and Liam Miller for part of the game, but you have to be in a winning position to do that.

'It's a good game for us simply because it's not one of these "past the post" results, but we are in a good, strong position and we don't want to surrender anything. Hopefully we can progress in Europe.'

Progress they did. But victory came at a price.

WEDNESDAY, 24 AUGUST 2005

UEFA Champions League, Third Qualifying Round (second leg)
Debreceni 0   Manchester United 3

UNITED: VAN DER SAR, NEVILLE (RICHARDSON 16), FERDINAND, BROWN, HEINZE, RONALDO, SCHOLES (BARDSLEY 46), FLETCHER (MILLER 61), GIGGS, SMITH, VAN NISTELROOY. SUBS NOT USED: HOWARD, PIQUE, PARK, ROONEY.

SCORERS:
Heinze 20, 61,
Richardson 65

ATTENDANCE:
27,000

The manager made five changes to Saturday's team. Gabriel Heinze, Wes Brown, Ryan Giggs and Alan Smith were given their first starts of the season and Cristiano Ronaldo also returned as Wayne Rooney, Mikael Silvestre, Roy Keane, John O'Shea and Ji-sung Park were left out.

It was a far from weakened side as United looked for the result that would take them into the competition proper. Sir Alex was anxious to avoid injuries, but with only a quarter of an hour gone it all turned pear-shaped: Gary Neville limped off with a groin strain.

'It's a typical injury from that kind of pitch, greasy and slippery, cut up badly. It's unusual for this time of the season, it was a winter pitch. Fortunately, we only got one injury out of it,' was Sir Alex's assessment.

Gabriel Heinze was the hero. The Argentinean scored twice with Kieran Richardson putting things beyond doubt with a great strike from the edge of the penalty area and the job was done.

Once back home it became apparent that Neville's injury was worse than anticipated, but that came as no surprise to Gary himself.

'I got the warning signs at the end of last season when I missed the FA Cup final. My groin had been niggling me and I knew what was coming because it had happened to me five years ago on my left side. This time, exactly the same thing was happening on my right.

'I felt really uncomfortable, but the scans weren't showing much. I knew what was coming. I had the injection in the summer, the same as I had five years ago, and the guy who did it said to me: "I would be very surprised if it doesn't go."

'I would have been amazed if it hadn't, knowing the symptoms and the discomfort I was getting. During the game it just went. It just tore on me and it was disappointing because I really wanted to stay fit and start the season strongly. I had felt good in pre-season, but on the other hand I was happy it was out of the way. I knew it had to go for me to be able to move on.'

He would be out of action for three months.

The game in Budapest meant that the Premiership fixture against newcomers Wigan, which appeared on the original listings, had to be re-scheduled. As they prepared for their next outing – a Sunday trip to Newcastle – United had already fallen behind leaders Chelsea, who had played a game more and who had a six-point advantage before the game got underway at St James', having played and won at Tottenham twenty-four hours earlier.

Before leaving for the Northeast, United also learned who their opponents would be in the group phase of the Champions League: French side Lille, Portuguese champions Benfica and Spain's Villarreal, who had seen off Everton in the qualifying stages.

'In assessing the difficulty of it against other groups then I don't think we can complain. Our hardest game will certainly be the first one against Villarreal away and the attraction for a lot of our fans will be the rekindling of memories when we play Benfica. We played Lille two or three years ago, but it is that type of group where we should do well, but where you've got difficult games,' said Sir Alex.

The manager also dealt with Neville's absence – 'Gary should be out for four to five weeks,' said Ferguson – by switching John O'Shea from left to right full back as 'Player of the Year' Gabi Heinze came in for his first Premiership start of the season.

The manager felt the trip to Tyneside was the toughest test so far.

'You always have to produce in Newcastle. We have to maximise our form at the moment, which I am pleased with, because it is good. It's a highly emotionally charged game at Newcastle, their fans are always up for it and it is a venue where you say to yourself "if we win there, it is a good one".

'It will be similar to Everton, although they have different styles of play and Newcastle have still got very good players. In the context of winning leagues you go to grounds and you prepare your way and don't worry too much about what Newcastle are going to be doing. It's up to us to maintain our form and show that form on Sunday, and we have got the players to do it.'

Sunday 28 August 2005

Barclays Premiership
Newcastle United 0   Manchester United 2

SCORERS:
Rooney 67,
Van Nistelrooy 90

UNITED: VAN DER SAR, O'SHEA, FERDINAND, SILVESTRE, HEINZE, FLETCHER (SMITH 85), KEANE (PARK 85), SCHOLES, RONALDO, ROONEY, VAN NISTELROOY. SUBS NOT USED: HOWARD, BROWN, GIGGS.

ATTENDANCE:
52,327

The Big Red Machine rolls on with Rooney and Ruud doing it again and the game living up to the pre-match build-up from Sir Alex.

United were boosted by the return of Roy Keane, who was joined by Wayne Rooney, John O'Shea and Mikael Silvestre amid rumblings from the Newcastle camp that this might be manager Graeme Souness's last game in charge, should they lose. Newcastle had new boy Albert Luque, signed from Deportivo La Coruna, in their line-up and his presence lifted the home fans, especially when he had the ball in the United net after only twelve minutes, only for his effort to be ruled offside.

It was after half time when the first goal came.

Wayne Rooney scored it in the sixty-seventh minute, forcing his way past an undecided Alain Boomsong, following a long clearance from van der Sar, and ramming his shot home. Newcastle held out as United created more chances, but had no answer to van Nistelrooy's clinical finishing as he scored virtually on the final whistle. It was Ruud's fourth of the season, edging him past partner Rooney in the goals chase and all thanks to an inch-perfect cross from Wayne.

With eleven goals scored in the first five fixtures, four of which he had scored himself, van Nistelrooy had reason for delight, but the striker was also swift to credit a defence that had yet to concede: 'We are looking fairly solid and that gives us a good feeling going into the games ahead.'

For fellow countryman Edwin van der Sar, playing for United was a new experience.

He appeared to have settled in quickly, but had it been easy for the 'keeper?

'No, not easy, you have to work hard for that. The quality in the group is very high and, of course, I'm experienced and know what's needed to perform in a high level and I did that and worked hard, and straight after the first couple of sessions I felt at home. We haven't conceded any goals, and that is the best start you could wish for after coming to a club like United.

'Things are different here. I think every club has its own specifics. I played at Juventus and that is also a big club, but it is a bit easier here because I can speak the language, whereas in Italy you have to experience things more for yourself with a new language, so it is much easier to come in here straightaway. Of course it's a massive club and every day you notice that.

'In Turin we had nothing like the United training centre. We used to train in their old stadium and we only had one pitch. I think they have changed it now and have got something like this, but I reckon United set the trend as far as the accommodation for training is concerned.'

For the millions who follow Manchester United, the thought of playing for the club is the stuff of dreams, but not it seems for

Edwin. As a boy, playing at Old Trafford was not a top priority.

'No, not really. You are always aware of the big names in football and when I left Ajax seven years ago there was some talk about me joining United, but it never came through. That's why I ended up in Italy, so I was just lucky to get the chance to finally come here.'

The first month of the season was over and even with their 100 per cent record, United had lost ground on Chelsea who had played and won a game more than the Reds.

United lay fourth in the table. Between them and the leaders were Charlton Athletic and their next Premiership opponents ... Manchester City.

CHAPTER THREE

The winning stops as injuries take their toll

It was hardly the best way to prepare for a derby game, with the majority of the squad whisked away on international duty almost as soon as the Newcastle game had ended. World Cup qualifiers beckoned, and Sir Alex was left alone with his thoughts as just four senior players reported for training at Carrington. Because of this he was unable to make any plans for the home game against Manchester City until he could check on who was available.

The troops began to return forty-eight hours before the kick-off.

Cristiano Ronaldo was a definite non-starter. His father had died and he had returned home to Portugal to be with his family. There were injury concerns too, but it soon became apparent that any patching up required might be more of a mental than a physical nature. England had beaten Wales in the first of their two fixtures, then lost 1–0 to Northern Ireland in Belfast.

'It's nice to get them back and they have come with varying degrees of success and failure, and that is something you have got to deal with. Our training sessions this week have been very sparse, but it was an important week for most of the players and a bad one for Rio and Wayne. Those two had the worst of the lot, which is something we have to deal with. Some will come back disappointed, some will come back pretty elated, but you hope the derby will give that edge to them.

'There are a few bumps and bruises and we are looking at the situation, but I think the nucleus of the squad will be okay,' said Sir Alex.

A pending suspension following a booking in Belfast meant that Wayne Rooney would miss England's next outing, but if he was feeling the pain, he hid it well.

'It was a disappointment to lose in Northern Ireland, but we have the chance to put it right in our next two games, which are both at Old Trafford and that means a good big pitch to play on. Old Trafford's great if you are the home team, but not so good coming here when you are the opposition, as I know from when I was with Everton. It can be quite daunting and going out there isn't a good experience, but when you are on the home side, the crowd are right behind you and it's a great stadium to play at.'

As derby day arrived, Wayne appeared on Man United Radio, the club's match-day station and was asked by presenter Matt Proctor to compare Manchester derbies to those of Merseyside.

'I think they are similar. They are both massive games and because it is the local rivals facing each other, everybody is right up for it. I came into the team last season and went into the Manchester derby and for me it was a different experience, but I could see what it meant to all the lads. You really want to win the game and we hope that by five o'clock tonight we can be leaving the ground on twelve points.'

For once City went into the game a point above United in the table. Like their neighbours they were undefeated, but they had also played a game more than the Reds.

'They seem to be doing all right, but we hope to take three points off them and get above them. They've had a good start and this is going to be a tough game,' Wayne added.

Sir Alex had his own view on why City had got off to such a good start under new manager Stuart Pearce.

'He's got them playing the way he played. They are aggressive and determined and he's got them organised. It has been a good start for them. Last season's game at Old Trafford was just a siege. We should have had two penalties, but when teams set out with a game plan like that, it's up to you to do something about it. It's no use saying they defended all day, it's not fair; you have got the ball at your feet all the time and it's up to you to create the chances and take them.'

SATURDAY 10 SEPTEMBER 2005

SCORER:
Van Nistelrooy 45
ATTENDANCE:
67, 839

Barclays Premiership
Manchester United 1   Manchester City 1

UNITED: VAN DER SAR, O'SHEA, FERDINAND, SILVESTRE, HEINZE, FLETCHER (KEANE 78), SMITH (RICHARDSON 87), SCHOLES, PARK (GIGGS 81), ROONEY, VAN NISTELROOY. SUBS NOT USED: HOWARD, BARDSLEY.

All things must end, but it was hard to take.

City snatched a point, might have stolen all three, and ended the Reds' winning run. Edwin van der Sar finally conceded a goal and he was far from happy with the outcome of the afternoon.

'Not conceding in our first four games, qualification for the Champions League and our opening league games, I was over the moon with that, but you knew that sooner or later you have to concede a goal. How unlucky it was it had to be against City.'

Sir Alex was more to the point.

'It was a ridiculous scoreline. They pulled everyone to the edge of their box, just as they did last season and looked for the scraps. They ended up scoring with their first shot. It is very frustrating, but that is football. It has happened before and it will happen again. You just have to accept it.'

The manager had stunned home fans by naming Roy Keane as one of his substitutes, but because he had a slight hamstring injury and, with away games coming up against Villarreal and Liverpool over the next eight days, Sir Alex wanted to save his skipper. He switched Alan Smith into an experimental central midfield role and things seemed to be working well.

It was Ruud van Nistelrooy who put the Reds in front just before half time, after City 'keeper David James fumbled a long-range free kick from Paul Scholes, but Joey Barton scored the equaliser midway through the second half and former Old Trafford favourite Andy Cole almost stole the show.

Seconds before the final whistle, the City striker found himself one-on-one with van der Sar, but the United 'keeper won the duel, magnificently blocking Cole's volley to prevent what would have certainly been a shock defeat.

Reflecting on what might have been, Ruud van Nistelrooy felt the Reds should have had more from Manchester's 133rd league derby:

'We have looked very confident from midfield to defence and that gives the strikers a great feeling to go for a goal late on, but there are times when we need to be a bit more direct. We cause problems when we get the ball straight to the forwards and perhaps we should be doing that a bit more.

'We played too many square balls after half time and we cannot afford too many more games like that because we need to win our home games. We don't want to give Chelsea too much of a lead, but on the positive side, despite the disappointing result, we are still looking fairly solid and that should give us a good feeling going into the games ahead.'

The draw meant that the gap between United and Chelsea was now five points, but Sir Alex remained optimistic.

'We have played only four games to Chelsea's five and it is very early yet. We are playing with great confidence and team spirit. We don't look like getting beaten either, so that is a good sign.'

There was little time to dwell on what might have been. The opening game of the Champions League was coming up and another former striker was waiting to face United. First Andy Cole, now Diego Forlan was getting ready for the Reds. The Uruguayan had left Old Trafford the previous season after failing to command a place in the side and became an instant hit with new club Villarreal.

His goals not only helped take them to fourth place in La Liga, but earned him equal standing in Europe's Golden Boot along with Arsenal's Thierry Henry – illustrious company for a player whose lasting claim to fame from a United viewpoint were the two goals he scored against Liverpool at Anfield in 2002. Sir Alex was looking forward to the reunion.

'Diego was a good little player, the problem was we didn't give him enough football. Because of the way we played and with us having Ruud van Nistelrooy, but his performances were fantastic. Because he was South American he found it difficult to be a sort of bit player, so that is the reason we let him go. We would have been happy to keep him, but the boy wanted to play.

'We haven't really kept in touch, but I did speak to him on his mobile a few months ago. He is in touch with all of the lads though and Albert the kit man as well – maybe he is still looking for free kit!'

The game would be the first ever meeting between United and the Spanish club.

'They have one or two important players, but Diego is the one who has got them into their present position. Don't get me wrong, I feel Riquelme is a fantastic player, but Diego's goals have been great for them. I was talking to his coach and he told me how much Diego raves about Manchester United and thinks we are a fabulous club, and he's telling all their players: "If you get a chance to go to Man United go!" That's nice and it's good of their coach to even admit that. He had a good time here and he was well liked by the fans. He is a great little lad and he was nothing but a good professional when he was here.'

One of Forlan's closest associates during his days at Old Trafford was skipper Keane. He took the Uruguayan under his wing after he had moved from Argentinean club Independiente in January 2002, but the two were robbed of the opportunity to meet up again, because when United flew out from Manchester Airport the day before the game, Keane was left behind.

He had aggravated a niggling hamstring problem after being sent on during the latter part of the derby, and with Liverpool next, the backroom staff were fighting to get him fit.

WEDNESDAY 14 SEPTEMBER 2005

UEFA Champions League, Group Stage
Villarreal 0   Manchester United 0

ATTENDANCE:
44,917

UNITED: VAN DER SAR, O'SHEA, FERDINAND, SILVESTRE, HEINZE (RICHARDSON 33),
FLETCHER, SCHOLES, SMITH, RONALDO (GIGGS 80), VAN NISTELROOY (PARK 80),
ROONEY. SUBS NOT USED: HOWARD, MILLER, BARDSLEY, PIQUE.

A valuable away point, but what a price to pay.

First Gabriel Heinze collapsed clutching his knee and had to be replaced, then United were forced to play the last half an hour with ten men when Wayne Rooney was sent off. He was shown the red card after sarcastically applauding Danish referee Kim Milton Nielsen while being booked for a challenge on Quique Alvarez. That meant backs-to-the-wall stuff until the final whistle.

The Spaniards were delighted with the stalemate after seeing United come close through Ruud van Nistelrooy, Paul Scholes and Mikael Silvestre, who all tested Villarreal's new 'keeper Mario Sebastian Viera, but the Reds also had luck on their side when a mix-up in the last minute led to Rio Ferdinand heading against his own crossbar. The Heinze blow came twelve minutes before the interval and at first no one knew the severity of the injury.

'We thought he may have twisted his knee, but it's not good news I'm afraid,' a devastated Sir Alex revealed. 'Gaby is going to be out for most of the season, he's got a cruciate knee injury. It is a bad blow out of such an innocuous incident. He went for a high ball and an opponent sort of knocked him from behind. In normal game situations nothing serious comes from that, but I think it is the way he landed that did the damage.

'We were in control of the game up to the time Wayne was sent off and after that we played sensibly. It didn't look as if we were going to lose and it turned out to be a reasonable result for us. We know now we must win our home games to qualify, but that has always been the rule and it won't change.'

Injuries were taking their toll: Louis Saha, Gary Neville, now Gabriel Heinze, but as Sir Alex would discover, things would get worse before they got better.

Without Heinze, the manager knew he had to make at least one change for the trip to Liverpool and had no hesitation turning to Kieran Richardson to take over at left full back. The young midfielder who kick-started his career with a loan spell with West Bromwich, helping to save them from relegation in 2005, had also earned himself a full England call-up. Now he had one from Sir Alex.

'You have to say the move to West Brom proved to be a real bonus. He came back to us a man and is showing great maturity now, even though he is only twenty. He does provide us with a different option as an attacking full-back and I am really pleased with him.'

Despite the setbacks, Sir Alex confessed that he was looking forward to what he claims is a bigger local derby than the one United had played the previous weekend.

'It never changes. I've been saying the same thing for the last eighteen years. It's a fantastic game in prospect every time you play them. Liverpool–United games are played in fantastic atmospheres. It's like a cauldron when you go to Anfield and our fans are always up for it when they come to Old Trafford. It's great. There is rivalry, but not that same tradition at places like Arsenal. The Arsenal game is always an important match, but to me the Liverpool game is still the biggest.

'It's down to the geographical situation, thirty-four miles apart, the history of both clubs – we are the most successful in Britain – then there is the rivalry between the fans. It's a fantastic fixture.'

Rio Ferdinand agreed.

'Because of our rivalry with Chelsea and Arsenal, people ask you whether the one with Liverpool has waned. Anyone who goes anywhere near that ground tomorrow will find out it hasn't. The fans of both sides will be up for it and there is no doubt in my mind that the players will be as well. We are fortunate to play football in all different parts of the world, but these are the atmospheres you will remember for the rest of your life. This game means so much to the fans and we know winning will make ours very happy indeed.'

SUNDAY 18 SEPTEMBER 2005

Barclays Premiership
Liverpool 0   Manchester United 0

ATTENDANCE:
44,917

UNITED: VAN DER SAR, O'SHEA, FERDINAND, SILVESTRE, RICHARDSON, SMITH, SCHOLES, KEANE (GIGGS 89), RONALDO (PARK 90), ROONEY (FLETCHER 88), VAN NISTELROOY. SUBS NOT USED: HOWARD, BARDSLEY.

Another draw, another injury.

This time it was Roy Keane, whose inclusion in the starting line-up had been a surprise. His recovery from the hamstring injury was kept a close secret, but there was no hiding his latest setback, as he became a member of the elite band of United stars to break a metatarsal on active service. In its time the foot injury has sidelined David Beckham, Gary Neville and Wayne Rooney, giving it almost designer status, but it was a major setback for the unlucky Keane. He tried to play through the pain after being hurt in a clash with Luis Garcia, but finally was forced to limp off in the eighty-ninth minute, to be told that around two months out of action lay ahead of him.

United went into the game in confident mood.

Why not? They had won on their last three visits to Anfield and beaten Liverpool in their two previous encounters, but this time it was a day of missed chances for both sides.

Ruud van Nistelrooy came closest to scoring in a tight first half, lobbing a Ferdinand throughball over the head of advancing 'keeper Jose Reina, but over the crossbar as well. There were bookings. Paul Scholes and Keane for United, Carragher and Traore for Liverpool, but it was the skipper's injury that stole the headlines.

'Roy is a big part of our team. To have him missing for two months is a massive disappointment for the team,' was how Wayne Rooney viewed things. 'But we have the players to come in and hopefully do the job for us. We've had a decent start to the season, we've had some tough away games and we're still unbeaten in the league. It's a decent start and hopefully it can continue. I suppose it's a good result for us going to Liverpool and getting a point, it is always tough coming here.'

Successive Premiership draws, while Chelsea kept winning, meant the gap at the top had increased to seven points with only five weeks of the season gone. Defensively, few could argue that United were looking stronger than they had since the days of Schmeichel, Bruce, Pallister and co. In the eight games played, they had conceded just one goal and Edwin van der Sar was earning the plaudits.

'Things are going OK, but we haven't won for the last three games, so it's important for the players to start winning again, starting with the game against Blackburn at the weekend. We have a game in hand on Chelsea, but we have to win that one yet and it's important that we start scoring again, because in the last couple of games we haven't created too many chances. We have worked hard on the pitch this week and we're going to get some more action.'

There was a six-day gap before the next game when Blackburn Rovers were due at Old Trafford and during the build-up many experts were forecasting a walkover for the Reds. Blackburn had made a poor start to the season: three defeats, two draws and just a single win from their first six games. It was also suggested that Rovers would take a defensive approach.

Edwin van der Sar spoke from experience as he previewed the encounter.

'That's nothing new. I think teams have come to United loads of times and played 4-5-1. I have been here a couple of times with Fulham and we have played like that, but the strikers just have to adjust and make sure that the chances you get, you put away.

'Hopefully we can pour some more misery on Blackburn because we need the three points and that's the only thing that is going to count. I've played against them a couple of times and we will have the video of them and the gaffer will take us through the tactics we are going to play. In Craig Bellamy they have a quality player who scored a couple of goals in their cup game in the week and I suppose he will be on his toes to try to get one at Old Trafford.'

The game also meant a return to Old Trafford for former favourite Mark Hughes, who would be hoping to get one over his mentor Sir Alex.

'Obviously, ex-player or whoever, I think every team wants to get something when they come here. We have to make sure that no club is going to get more points here this season than they did last,' said the 'keeper.

Blackburn had drawn 0–0 on their last visit so the only way to better that performance was by winning. They did!

Saturday 24 September 2005

Barclays Premiership
Manchester United 1   Blackburn Rovers 2

SCORER:
Van Nistelrooy 67
ATTENDANCE:
67,765

UNITED: VAN DER SAR, O'SHEA (BARDSLEY 57), FERDINAND, SILVESTRE, RICHARDSON, FLETCHER (ROONEY 55), SMITH, SCHOLES, RONALDO, VAN NISTELROOY, PARK (GIGGS 69). SUBS NOT USED: HOWARD, MILLER.

Shocks all round. First, Wayne Rooney was left on the bench at the start, then Blackburn took everyone by surprise, including Sir Alex.

'I expected them to come here and try to stifle the game, but in fairness they played with a positive attitude and I can't deny them their victory. They tried to win, but if you had told me we were going to create eight chances in the first half of a home game I would be delighted. Then, if you said we would miss eight I would say there were danger signs there. Don't hit the target and you have absolutely no complaints and you know exactly what the problem is.'

He explained that Rooney was left out of the starting line-up because of the two-game suspension imposed on him after being sent off in Spain. With Roy Keane also out of contention, the manager saw it as an opportunity to field the line-up he would use in the Champions League game against Benfica in three days' time.

'We would have preferred to play Wayne, but we have to be fair to the members of the squad who are going to replace him on Tuesday and that was the reason,' he said, after drafting in Darren Fletcher and Ji-sung Park.

They could do little to prevent the upset, as two goals from Morten Gamst Pedersen earned Blackburn their win. His first was a free kick that floated over van der Sar and inside the far post, the second coming nine minutes from time, after an uncharacteristic mistake from Paul Scholes, who gave the ball away inside his own half.

Rooney came on in the second half and quickly linked up with Ruud van Nistelrooy who scored a sixty-seventh minute equaliser, but joy was short-lived and Mark Hughes became the first Blackburn manager to chalk up a win at Old Trafford for forty-three years.

The frustration of the afternoon left some supporters far from happy. As the players left the pitch and Sir Alex and his backroom staff walked towards the dressing room, some fans above the tunnel at the Stretford End began booing. It was no mass demonstration, with most of the boos drowned out by other fans, but the incident was captured by television cameras, screened in newsrooms around the country and consequently spilled onto the back pages the following morning.

It was hardly the build-up United wanted ahead of an important Champions League clash and comments from the Benfica camp stirred things up more. Striker Simao Sabrosa reckoned Benfica's spies at the Blackburn game had seen enough to give them hope of adding to United's woes.

'Manchester United are not at their best at the moment and it is a great opportunity for Benfica. The great advantage we have is the mistakes being made by their defenders. Edwin van der Sar is a better goalkeeper than they had before, but they make so many errors in defence it does not matter. They are now under pressure and we know that. A United without Keane, Heinze, Neville and Rooney is one that can be beaten.'

Darren Fletcher had other ideas.

'There was a lot of disappointment after the defeat on Saturday and I thought it was a game we didn't deserve to lose. There is still a long way to go and we're confident in our ability and we'll be there at the end of the season challenging. But you can't look back. You have to look forward to the next game and that's Benfica. There's a lot of history between the clubs and it's going to be a special night ... but only if we win.

'We haven't faced them before in the Champions League, but we hear they're a good side. I suppose they are still a bit of an unknown quantity, but I'm sure everyone will do their homework and we will have a good idea about them before we go out there. At Old Trafford we are capable of beating anybody and that is what we'll be trying to do.'

Older fans knew the Benfica of the past.

Names like Eusebio, Torres and Coluna conjured up memories of 1968 when Bobby Charlton, George Best and Brian Kidd had grounded the mighty Eagles from Lisbon as United became the first English side to win the European Cup.

The Benfica of today were the reigning Portuguese champions and were coached by Dutch legend Ronald Koeman. They were a mystery to some perhaps, but not Carlos Queiroz, who warned of the threat from his fellow countrymen.

'We expect this team to come here playing with some precautions. They will know they are playing Manchester United at Old Trafford and have to be defensive, but Benfica are a team with attacking players and we expect that when they have the ball they will try to create something special.

'They are quick and skilful, so when you have a team like that you always expect quality football. They have Brazilians, Portuguese, Italians in their line-up and the big threats will come from Simao, Geovanni, the ex-Barcelona player and Fabrizio Miccoli, who are really good attacking players.

'Knowing Koeman and that the team is doing well – they have won their last three games – they won't change their style of play away from home, but we won't be changing our approach either. We will use the strengths we have at the moment and what's important is that during the game we are dominant.'

On Monday 26 September, the day before the game, Sir Alex took his seat at the Champions League press conference to find the media had another agenda. They wanted his reaction to Saturday's boo-boys and mounting speculation about his future.

'I don't want to talk about myself. What has happened in the past doesn't matter. Tomorrow's game is the most important thing and we are doing a good job getting the players back from Saturday's defeat. European nights have always been special at Old Trafford; in my experience they have always had an extra edge. I am sure the supporters will be great.'

He was right.

Old Trafford staged a sixties nostalgia night as United faced their old foes for the first time in thirty-seven years. Even the cover of the match programme was a flashback – a reproduction of that sold at Wembley in 1968 – and just like Sir Matt all those years ago when Sir Alex stepped out, it was to rapturous applause.

The stadium rose with supporters unanimously pledging their faith in the man who had taken the club to so much success and letting the dissatisfied minority know their feelings.

'Stand up, if you love Fergie,' was the chorus; a smile and a wave was the response.

TUESDAY 27 SEPTEMBER 2005

SCORERS:
Giggs 39,
Van Nistelrooy 85

ATTENDANCE:
66,112

UEFA Champions League, Group Stage
Manchester United 2   Benfica 1

UNITED: VAN DER SAR, BARDSLEY, FERDINAND, O'SHEA, RICHARDSON, FLETCHER, SMITH, SCHOLES, RONALDO, GIGGS, VAN NISTELROOY. SUBS NOT USED: HOWARD, PIQUE, MILLER, PARK, EBANKS-BLAKE, ROSSI.

At last! September ends with a win and, fittingly, with so much emphasis on that long-gone night in May 1968 when youthful left winger John Aston ran rings around Benfica, it was Ryan Giggs –

starting only his second game of the season – who scored the opener.

There was a touch of luck about it. Ryan's first-half free kick deflected off defender Nelson before landing beyond the reach of Jose Moreira, but it sent an explosion of relief ripping round Old Trafford.

Benfica refused to lie down. They came out in the second period looking for an equaliser and got it through that man Simao whose pre-match proclamation, 'Old Trafford holds no fear for us,' was no hollow boast. His fifty-ninth minute free kick, awarded for a foul by Alan Smith on Miccoli, was perfection: the ball flying into the top corner and giving van der Sar no chance.

Then Scholes went close, Ronaldo missed and Benfica threatened. Enter Ruud van Nistelrooy.

With five minutes remaining, a Giggs corner dropped in the box and the Dutch master scored. Two Champions League games played, one drawn, one won: after all the fuss, it was a satisfactory start to any European campaign.

Ruud was centre of attraction backstage: 'After that equaliser some people probably thought "here we go again", but we made sure we got the three points. It was good to get a goal quite late on and a great feeling all round the stadium, which was fantastic for all of the game. The fans were very supportive from minute one right till the end and they helped us through it. We dominated most of the game apart from the period after they had scored. It was a good day for us.'

Another to warrant attention was debutant full-back Phil Bardsley: 'I was delighted to get a run out and equally delighted for the lads to get such a great result because we needed that tonight. You always have to be patient in Europe. I have watched it for a few years now and you follow from the older players who set a great example, and I think we adapted well.

'You have to try to enjoy it as much as you can. We had to dig in, but full credit to the lads, we did and we got a great result. It was hard, but I think we were in control of the game, so in that sense we had to show our character after they scored and we did.'

There was more to the win than that according to Alan Smith. Next day, as physio staff eased the aches and pains at Carrington and the players began their preparations for the weekend trip to Fulham, the striker-turned-midfielder revealed that the weekend's demonstration of dissent had not gone unnoticed in the dressing room.

'If people think when we walked off the pitch on Saturday we just forgot about that result they are wrong. We spoke about it on Sunday morning, and it wasn't nice. We let ourselves down and we let everybody connected with the club down. The criticism hurt and sometimes you need to take it personally. But you don't get anything by feeling sorry for yourself.

'Sometimes you learn more from defeats, because victories just cover over the cracks. The gaffer asked for his big players to stand up and be counted. I know people have been questioning our spirit over the last few weeks – but if the team spirit had not been good and if there had not been some determined characters in the team we would have gone down after Benfica equalised.

'It is as simple as that. In the face of adversity, you see who your big players are. Maybe we chased the ball a bit too much in the five or ten minutes immediately after their goal, but that was only because we wanted to win so much. It just shows how together we are.

'We play football for the team and the manager. We have world-class players – and whatever formation the manager wants us to play, we should be able to play it and play it right. Maybe we got a bit more support to Ruud, which is something we have been working on.

'People criticised us on Saturday, but the first half last night was our best performance of the season. We created nineteen chances and we should have taken more of them than we did.'

Reminded it was his tackle which led to the Benfica equaliser, he added: 'It was a nightmare for me, because the last thing the boss said to me before I went out was "don't give a free kick away in that area". As soon as I did it I thought, "Somebody get me out of this!"

Thankfully, Ruud did. Everyone knows this is his competition. He has scored a lot of vital goals at vital times for this club – and he did it again.'

That night Roy Keane appeared on MUTV and caused a shock. It became clear, despite the manager's many claims he would be given the chance to extend his playing career with United beyond the summer of 2006, that the Irishman had other plans.

'I would like to play another year or two, but I do not think it will be at Manchester United. I would be surprised if I was offered a new contract and even if I was, I would not expect it to be until the end of the season, but by then I will have already made a decision about what I am going to do.

'There comes a time for everybody when they have to move on and I am prepared to play elsewhere. I think it will be good to experience a different dressing room. It wouldn't be an English team though, coming back to Old Trafford and going into the away dressing room would be too hard for me to stomach. My gut reaction last season was this would be my last year and I still feel that way. You have to learn and be prepared to move on. Life will not stop when I leave Manchester United.

'It might be an opportunity to go into management or coaching somewhere else and it is best to make a clean break, because coaching at Manchester United doesn't really appeal. I don't want to look too far ahead because I want to play on for a bit yet, but I wouldn't want to drop too far down. Your first job in management is an important one. I would like to go to a club with ambition, a decent fan base and some decent players,' he said.

His words hit the tabloids and, before the players set off for London for the Fulham game, Carlos Queiroz found himself facing a barrage of unwanted questions. He was standing in for the manager at the pre-match press conference because Sir Alex had another engagement.

'First of all we need to concentrate on our priorities. We have games to play, players to recover from injury situations and, as usual, the manager, at the right time, in the right way, will address that situation. The right way would be in a private and confidential way so we don't discuss these things in public.'

Would Roy be difficult to replace?

'I have this personal view. You don't replace Pele; you don't replace Maradona, Eusebio, Roy Keane. You just create new players in new teams.'

Carlos himself had been in the news during the week. According to reports, he had told a Portuguese newspaper that those United supporters who had chanted '4-4-2' during the Blackburn game, in a bid to get Sir Alex to change the formation, were 'stupid'.

The story had hit the headlines on the day of the Benfica game, but according to Sir Alex's assistant there had been an almighty mix-up. So much so that the newspaper's editor had written to him to put things straight.

In an unusual move the club released details of the letter along with an official statement. The editor wrote: 'Only a bad translation service could have allowed the phrase that you used to describe the wide range of criticism that football can be subjected to – from stupidity to imagination – could have been transformed into a criticism of Manchester United fans. This serious misinterpretation of your words caused great perplexity as your current statements (and those in the past) have shown your position to always be one where managers should respect criticism from the fans.'

Carlos himself added: 'I want to address some words to the fans. Before the incident in the English press, I thought Manchester United fans were the best in the world and after the Benfica game I am sure of that because they didn't fall into the trap. They reacted fantastically. They gave great support to me and I want to show all my gratitude, because after what had happened it was not so easy to have such a fantastic reaction. I hope everybody will forget this incident and learn from something, because words can kill as well.'

And what about that game tomorrow?

'It will be very intensive, professional, both teams need to win. It will be a really tough game because both teams want to win but more than that, we need to win.'

SATURDAY 1 OCTOBER 2005

Barclays Premiership
Fulham 2 Manchester United 3

UNITED: VAN DER SAR, O'SHEA, FERDINAND, SILVESTRE, RICHARDSON (BARDSLEY 57), PARK, FLETCHER, SMITH, GIGGS (RONALDO 77), ROONEY, VAN NISTELROOY (SCHOLES 83). SUBS NOT USED: HOWARD, PIQUE.

SCORERS:
Van Nistelrooy 16 (pen), 44, Rooney 18

ATTENDANCE:
21,862

Needs must. With Wayne Rooney available, Sir Alex made changes to the midweek line-up. Mikael Silvestre was back after missing the Champions League game through injury, Ryan Giggs came in for his first Premiership start of the season and was handed the skipper's armband and Sir Alex also opted for Ji-sung Park and Darren Fletcher ahead of Cristiano Ronaldo and Paul Scholes.

United were desperate to claw back lost ground, but what a way to start. Within a minute they were a goal down with Collins John ruining Edwin van der Sar's return to his former club.

'It was a terrific game. End to end, and Fulham played a great part in that,' said Sir Alex after witnessing a remarkable turnaround.

Ji-sung Park stole the show. The South Korean won a penalty in the sixteenth minute when Moritz Volz brought him down and Ruud van Nistelrooy fired home to equalise and two minutes later United led. This time Rooney scored, following some good work from Park, but with less than half an hour gone, back came Fulham, and a goal from Claus Jensen made it game on.

'They got a break for the first goal in a scramble between Rio and John. The second goal looked like really slack defending by us. It went straight in – just like last weekend,' said the boss.

The winner came before half time. Park broke forward, crossed to the feet of van Nistelrooy, whose tap home was a formality. That was that, and Sir Alex was smiling.

'Fulham are a real handful. They played exceptionally well against Tottenham on Monday night and didn't get anything for it. They played well again today and didn't get anything for it. But, equally, some of our football was scintillating in the first half. Park was excellent; the boy is coming on terrifically. His movement off the ball and his awareness of space is exceptional for a young man.'

As United travelled north, Wayne Rooney spoke about the transformation in the camp and how there was still confidence that Chelsea could be caught.

'Two wins in five days has changed the feeling. Everything gets blown out of all proportion here anyway, but it is still early days. We will keep trying to win all our games and see what happens.'

It was time for another international break, with Wayne ready to join up with the rest of the England squad ahead of games at Old Trafford against Austria and Poland. He would miss the first through suspension, but not the vital qualifier against Poland.

By the time the party reached Manchester, news had broken that George Best had been admitted to hospital earlier that day suffering from 'flu-like' symptoms. The former United star was in the intensive care unit of Cromwell Hospital in west London, but was said to be in a stable condition.

Because Old Trafford was being used for the England games, the international squad trained at Carrington, so it was familiar surroundings for the United contingent, with Sir Alex also able to keep a careful eye on things.

There were the usual concerns before the next Premiership outing with Ji-sung Park returning from a fourteen-hour trip with South Korea, while Ryan Giggs reported a tight hamstring after playing for Wales. A major blow was that Kieran Richardson had to be ruled out of the trip to Sunderland.

'Kieran had a tight thigh muscle before he went off to the England squad and he never said anything to anyone at the club. It's his enthusiasm to go and play for his country that's cost us really. England recognised it, sent him for a scan on the Monday, nothing really showed up. He tried jogging on the Tuesday and they just sent him back to us, so I think he'll be out for seven to ten days.

'That rules him out of tomorrow where we expect a battle, but you will always get that because they are trying to survive in the

Premiership. It isn't easy after coming out of the First Division. There are some glimmers of hope for them in that Wigan have done exceptionally well and so have West Ham, and Sunderland being the other promoted side will be saying, "if they can do it, we can do it."

'It'll be a full house because it's United in town and a tough game, but we know these are bridges you've got to cross in the course of a full season.'

Saturday 15 October 2005

Barclays Premiership
Sunderland 1   Manchester United 3

UNITED: VAN DER SAR, BARDSLEY, FERDINAND, SILVESTRE, O'SHEA (PIQUE 89), PARK, SCHOLES, SMITH, RONALDO (MILLER 89), ROONEY, VAN NISTELROOY (ROSSI 78). SUBS NOT USED: HOWARD, FLETCHER.

SCORERS:
Rooney 40,
Van Nistelrooy 76,
Rossi 87

ATTENDANCE:
39,085

The accent was on youth, with United's travelling support given a taste of things to come. Before kick-off, Sir Alex had announced that both John O'Shea and Darren Fletcher had signed four-year contract extensions: 'We're all delighted. It represents our vision of the young players being with the club for a long time, which is something the support recognises and appreciates, and it gives us a foundation from which we can work for the next few years to keep a group of players together and try and maintain the success we have had over the past fifteen years.'

Before the game ended, the manager had unleashed another youngster on the big stage. United took the lead just before half time when Ronaldo broke and crossed into Rooney's path and he hammered home an angled drive.

Sunderland pushed for an equaliser, but in the seventy-sixth minute another United counter-attack led to the second goal. Rooney sent van Nistelrooy away and he drove his shot under a diving Kelvin Davis. Even at 2-0 down Sunderland refused to give in. With eight minutes left, Stephen Elliott scored from long range, but it was substitute Giuseppe Rossi who made it his day.

The teenager had replaced van Nistelrooy shortly before Sunderland scored and as the home side threatened to pull level, he tied up the points after picking up a loose ball and hammering home a shot from twenty-five yards. The new kid had arrived on the United block.

'It was a special moment for me because I scored. It was something I won't forget because it was always my dream to make my debut and to score a goal and it happened. You just want to score goals, and that's my target in every game and I was lucky enough to get one. What I remember most is all the players jumping on me after the goal, but it was something very nice for me,' Rossi recalled, once he had regained his breath.

The American–Italian, still four months away from his nineteenth birthday, had scored for Manchester United and because of the goal Gerard Pique – a day younger than his close pal – also got a taste of the action.

'I was about to go on when Sunderland scored so, because it was 2–1, the manager told me to stay where I was. Then when Giuseppe got his goal he let me go on, so I have to say thank you to him. You always want to play in the Premiership, that's your dream and you cannot explain with words how you feel when you enter the pitch because not a lot of people can do that. You are privileged and it is great, and you have to enjoy it, but that's difficult because you're a little bit nervous obviously.'

'This could be the starting point of our careers,' Rossi added. 'So it was good for me and for him, and we just hope to build on it.'

For Pique, who joined United from Barcelona, it was time to thank a few of his senior colleagues. 'Rio and Mikael, Wes and Sheasy all try to help me and I think it's good because Sheasy and Wes came from the Academy, through the reserves and they can help in terms of how to get the experience, what you have to do when you are a teenager. They are also internationals, so it's great experience for you training and playing with them.

'I haven't set myself any targets. I haven't said I want to arrive in the first team this year or next year, it doesn't matter. We are both doing very well and are on our way and if things continue like this I think we are in a great position to be in the squad soon. We have to enjoy that.'

Like Gerard, Giuseppe also has a mentor at the club. 'I look up to Ruud van Nistelrooy because he plays in my role and he is a great goalscorer, one of the best in the world. Getting information from him is great and I just want to keep doing my best here at United.'

Van Nistelrooy was a proud man. 'I was on the bench at the time and I wanted to go on the pitch to celebrate with him, but the fourth official stopped me and told me I'd get booked if I went on! He's a great talent and a great character as well, and I was so happy to see him get a goal on his Premiership debut.

'Rossi has impressed a lot of people and I was so happy to see him score. He puts a lot of hard work into his game in training and he thoroughly deserves his goal. We talk about things and because of the position he plays he wants to know stuff from me. He asks me questions and I always try to help him. He has been impressing people in the reserves and all of us in training and he deserves great credit for that.'

Smiles all round, but there was little time to enjoy the moment.

Another Champions League game was looming against French side Lille. United were hot favourites to win and enhance their start to the group phase, but once again matters elsewhere dominated the start of the UEFA pre-match press conference. Reports that Sir Alex was on the shortlist to replace Brian Kerr as manager of the Republic of Ireland national side had filled every sports page for days.

There were claims the story had been given credence because it had allegedly originated in an article written by former United star Denis Irwin. Facing the media in Old Trafford's Europa Suite, Sir Alex opened with a firm denial.

'I don't know where they have got the story from, because Denis Irwin hasn't spoken to anyone about this. He doesn't know where it has come from. It's the usual nonsense, but I made the point last week, I have heard about it, but I have no idea how it came about.

They have even mentioned me for the England job.

'Listen. When I am finished here, I am finished. There won't be another club. You don't leave Man United and go anywhere else. This is the best place. There won't be any other club ... or country after this job, I'm finished. I think it's important to clarify that because Ireland have got a manager and I don't think it's nice when you see yourself being linked with a job that somebody is already in.'

That evening Denis Irwin used one of his regular MUTV appearances to put the matter straight. He announced that he had apologised to his ex-boss while accepting responsibility for the article which appeared in his name adding: 'I was disappointed to read the comments because it was a lot of nonsense. If anybody knows me, I have the least interest in the political side of football. Someone got carried away and the piece didn't go out the way I wanted it to. But it is my fault and I have to live with it.'

If Irwin was red faced, he was not alone the following night.

TUESDAY 18 OCTOBER 2005

ATTENDANCE:
60,626

UEFA Champions League, Group Stage
Manchester United 0   Lille 0

UNITED: VAN DER SAR, BARDSLEY, FERDINAND, SILVESTRE, O'SHEA, RONALDO, FLETCHER, SCHOLES, SMITH, GIGGS (PARK 83), VAN NISTELROOY. SUBS NOT USED: HOWARD, PIQUE, MILLER, MARTIN, ROSSI, EBANKS-BLAKE.

For the second time in three European games United were reduced to ten men. They also found themselves held to a goalless draw after another frustrating ninety minutes, with doubts starting to rise about them making progress in the competition. They stayed top of their group thanks only to a similar stalemate in Spain, where Benfica held Villarreal 1-1, but the home fans had little to shout about after seeing Paul Scholes sent off for picking up two yellow cards and a Rooney-less attack produce a toothless performance.

Rio Ferdinand did not hide his feelings as the French celebrated:

Two midfield titans, Roy Keane and Steven Gerrard, clash in the game at Anfield. No one knew it then, but the broken metatarsal Roy picked up would mean that he had played his last game for United.

Ruud van Nistelrooy finishes off a United move to help the Reds draw level against Blackburn Rovers. But with the injury list mounting, the defeat left them trailing Chelsea by ten points at the end of September.

Ryan Giggs, starting for only the second time all season, celebrates his goal against Benfica with Phil Bardsley. Astonishingly, it was to be United's only victory in the group.

Ji-sung Park is tripped to earn United a penalty against Fulham. With the Korean also setting up two further goals, it was his best performance so far in a United shirt.

'Giuseppe Rossi came on for his Premiership debut with less than fifteen minutes left against Sunderland. But it was all the eighteen-year-old needed to score a goal, a special moment I won't forget.'

Ryan Giggs in action in the Champions League against Lille in October. What should have been a special occasion for him – his 100th European appearance – was marred by a fractured cheekbone.

John O'Shea tussles with Jermain Defoe during the October draw against Spurs. With United slipping down to fifth in the table, he said: 'We have to worry about our own results.'

The third round of the Carling Cup against Barnet was an opportunity to bring in some new players. Sylvan Ebanks-Blake makes the most of his chance, scoring the fourth goal at the end of the game.

'It was disappointing we didn't win the game, but circumstances changed things on the night. Scholesy was sent off quite undeservedly. It seemed like a game in which you weren't allowed to tackle and it was the referee who made it that way. I don't like to get on the backs of referees because they have a hard enough job, but he was whistle happy all night and it seemed too easy for him to blow for any challenge.

'If we could have got an early goal it might have changed the face of the game. They would have had to come out of their shell and play against us, but as it was they sat back a little bit and were very disciplined in their game plan.

'We know we have the quality of players upfront who, if they get a chance, will normally put them away, but today it wasn't the case. We'll be looking to improve on that, but when we saw that Villarreal and Benfica had drawn, it kind of went for us. We have been let off the hook a little bit, but you want to win your home games and that wasn't the case tonight.

'You know you are going to miss someone like Wayne Rooney, he's a fantastic player, but we have others who can come in and do a job. Today, though, we didn't hit the spark we were looking for, but that isn't just down to one player being out. We won't make excuses because we have the talent in the club to go out and get the results we need.'

If the result was bad, there was an even bigger blow for United. Ryan Giggs, who again captained the team – this time on his 100th European appearance – was involved in an incident midway through the second half.

'I went up for a header and got an elbow right on the cheekbone. I knew something was wrong straightaway, but the referee came over and didn't say much really other than tell me to get up. I was expecting him to see something on my face. I tried to carry on for four or five minutes then my right eye was getting blurred so I called the physio and told him I couldn't carry on.

'As soon as I came off, the doctor saw the depression in my cheek and knew what had happened straightaway. I was gutted. I had already had a stop-start season, having had a virus at the beginning which made me miss the first few games, so it was really disappointing knowing I was going to be out for six or seven weeks.'

'We didn't realise until we brought him off that he had fractured his cheekbone,' Sir Alex revealed three days later when the full extent of the injury was known. 'It's a pretty horrible one really. He's getting operated on this morning and in actual fact has three fractures in his cheekbone, so it'll be plated.

'When you see replays of the incident, I was amazed the referee didn't allow the physiotherapist to come on. Our doctor is not happy about it. If we had been able to get on the pitch we would have taken him off immediately, because you could see the indentation in his cheek and there could have been something serious there.

'The miracle is, and we are really fortunate in that respect, Ryan didn't get another knock on it or something serious could have happened. It's down to his own courage that he stayed on. It's another injury we could do without, but it's just unfortunate when these things happen to you.

'We had a spell two years ago similar to this and seven or eight years ago there was another terrible spell when Arsenal beat us on the run-in. But we have to go on and there is no way you can sit down and contemplate picking a team without thinking about winning. Tomorrow against Tottenham, we'll have changes, but we'll also have the same winning mentality we always have. That's the way Manchester United has to be. We are judged not on what the team is, but the result.'

As if the injuries were not enough, there was another cloud hanging over the club. Cristiano Ronaldo had been questioned by police following allegations he had sexually assaulted a woman in a London hotel. It would be some weeks before it emerged that the Portuguese star had been wrongly accused and all charges against him dropped, but Sir Alex found himself dealing a sensitive situation.

'He's had a difficult time, but he trained yesterday and he'll train today and he'll be OK,' said the manager.

Seven experienced first teamers were now out of contention for the visit of an in-form Tottenham, and that was the last thing United wanted. Spurs were going well, second in the table, a point ahead of the Reds, but nine behind Chelsea. Both sides desperately needed to win.

Saturday 22 October 2005

Barclays Premiership
Manchester United 1   Tottenham Hotspur 1

UNITED: VAN DER SAR, BARDSLEY (ROSSI 82), FERDINAND, SILVESTRE, O'SHEA, FLETCHER (RONALDO 77), SMITH, SCHOLES, ROONEY, VAN NISTELROOY, PARK. SUBS NOT USED: HOWARD, MILLER, PIQUE.

SCORER:
Silvestre 7

ATTENDANCE:
67,856

Last season, this fixture was crammed with controversy; television proved Spurs were robbed of a goal when Roy Carroll dragged a Pedro Mendes shot back from the wrong side of his goal line, while United were also denied what looked like a blatant penalty as it finished 0–0.

This time, another stalemate had dark clouds gathering.

Home form was the big problem. Three games, three goals and four points in the Premiership, while away from Old Trafford it was a totally different situation. United had scored ten goals on their travels and won thirteen points, but again it was missed chances that cost the Reds. They took the game by the throat from the opening minute and went ahead in the seventh before throwing it away in second half.

Wayne Rooney, in magnificent form, contributed to United's goal. His pressure led to a free kick, which Paul Scholes took and, as Ruud van Nistelrooy headed down and Spurs 'keeper Paul Robinson spilled, Mikael Silvestre slid in to score.

In the quest for a second Alan Smith went close, so did van Nistelrooy and substitute Ronaldo, but Spurs equalised in the seventy-second minute when Rio Ferdinand bundled over Jenas and the midfielder converted the resulting free kick.

*

It was a crucial result, with both clubs missing the chance to make ground on Chelsea who next day dropped their first points of the season when they drew 1–1 at Everton. Instead United slipped to fifth, finding themselves a point behind Wigan, with Charlton stepping above Spurs into second place. According to the bookmakers both of them could forget the title, but John O'Shea had a different point of view. He reckoned United should forget Chelsea.

'We have to concentrate on ourselves and worry about our own results, especially at Old Trafford. The margin for error is getting less. Look at the sides around us. Wigan won again and that just shows the competitiveness of the Premiership. All we can do is keep focusing on the next game. We have another tough away match at Middlesbrough on Saturday and we have to get the three points. The lads have to stick together, stand up and be counted.

'At this club, we are expected to go out and win every game. Anyone who thinks it doesn't matter when we don't do that should see the arguments we have in the dressing room and on the training ground when we are talking about things that could have been done better.

'We are always disappointed not to win matches when we should have. We had a golden opportunity to control the Spurs game, but we needed the second goal to kill it off and games can swing on one moment. The free kick Jenas scored was an absolutely fantastic hit and that knocked us back a bit. We know we need to beat Chelsea in a fortnight, but the most important match ahead of us just now is Middlesbrough.'

There was another game before that, and the chance for the younger players to show that playing at Old Trafford was no problem.

In the third round of the Carling Cup, United were drawn against League Two side Barnet, but Sir Alex's plan of giving Louis Saha his first run-out had to be scrapped when the striker picked up another injury. Instead the manager turned to Giuseppe Rossi and Cambridge-born striker Sylvan Ebanks-Blake to lead the attack, and the move paid off.

WEDNESDAY 26 OCTOBER 2005

Carling Cup, Third Round
Manchester United 4   Barnet 1

UNITED: HOWARD, BARDSLEY, BROWN, PIQUE, ECKERSLEY, MARTIN (GIBSON 75), MILLER, R. JONES, RICHARDSON, ROSSI, EBANKS-BLAKE. SUBS NOT USED: STEELE, SMITH, PARK, SILVESTRE.

SCORERS:
Miller 4,
Richardson 19,
Rossi 51,
Ebanks-Blake 89

ATTENDANCE:
43,673

This was the night the Theatre of Dreams turned into a Palace of Nightmares for Barnet goalkeeper Ross Flitney. It should have been the game of his life, but instead it became one he would rather forget and all because of a horrendous howler two minutes after the start. He was sent off for handling the ball outside his area.

Referee Richard Beeby stuck to the letter of the law when Flitney came out too far to collect a harmless throughball, but if that was bad luck, what about team-mate Louie Soares. He had to be sacrificed by manager Paul Fairclough to make way for substitute goalkeeper Scott Tynan after hardly touching the ball. Things got worse.

The first thing Tynan did was to pick the ball out of his net after Liam Miller brilliantly bent home the free kick and, not surprisingly, it all proved too much for Barnet. Ten men could not handle a ten-change United, who followed up with goals from Richardson, Rossi and Ebanks-Blake. Dean Sinclair earned some consolation by scoring late on for the Bees.

Coincidence? Luck? In the light of events to follow, someone certainly had a touch of foresight while selecting material for the Barnet match programme. Inside the front cover was a picture of Roy Keane relaxed and smiling in the MUTV studio promoting an article billed as: 'The skipper unplugged, frank, uncompromising and revealing.'

October ended with a trip to Teesside where Sir Alex had the chance to renew acquaintances with former assistant Steve McClaren. He had been at United during the most successful period of the club's history, arriving from Derby in the January of 1999 and sharing in the Treble-winning campaign that season. McClaren was with the Reds as they went on to win the Premiership for the next three seasons, the only club to have done this since the new league was launched, then left to try his hand as manager of Middlesbrough.

Sir Alex reckoned some of his methods had rubbed off on his former right-hand man. 'I think Steve may have picked up on the way we operate here. His youth set-up is very good. That's important and over the last two or three years Middlesbrough have done very well on that front. The other thing that we do at United is give these young players a chance.'

SATURDAY 29 OCTOBER 2005

SCORER:
Ronaldo 90

ATTENDANCE:
30,579

Barclays Premiership
Middlesbrough 4   Manchester United 1

UNITED: VAN DER SAR, BARDSLEY (RICHARDSON 31), FERDINAND (BROWN 87), O'SHEA, SILVESTRE, FLETCHER, SMITH, SCHOLES, PARK (RONALDO 60), ROONEY, VAN NISTELROOY. SUBS NOT USED: HOWARD, ROSSI.

It was a reunion to forget for Sir Alex. He found this unlikely hammering hard to take and hardly the way to build up to the next Premiership game against leaders Chelsea. 'It was shocking. On today's form, we couldn't beat anybody!' he said.

Edwin van der Sar was equally stunned and swift to shoulder blame for a second-minute blunder that gifted Gaizka Mendieta Boro's opener. 'The ball swirled a little, but I should have saved it. That is not a good situation to start with, and it all started to go wrong from that goal. It hurts quite a lot. It is a team game, but we made a lot of individual errors and that cost us dearly. There is not much we can say, and I don't have to tell you what the manager was like after the game. It is quite obvious how he and the players feel.

'We are not in the greatest spirit at the moment, but we have to analyse what went wrong and somehow start to focus on Wednesday's game against Lille. Hopefully we can pick up something from that game, which we can take into the Chelsea match.'

After seeing Jimmy Floyd Hasselbaink add a second, a Yakubu penalty make it 3–0 at half time and then Mendieta put the finishing touch to Boro's amazing display in the seventy-sixth minute, Sir Alex did not try to hide his feelings.

'We are still scrambling away trying to get some consistency into our game, but it just has not happened. People are talking about Chelsea, but we have to look after our own results and they have not been good enough. Like everyone else, we have been hoping Chelsea drop points. We weren't intending to give them any.

'We were on the back foot immediately and never recovered, and the second and third goals were terrible ones to lose. You can't afford to do that at this level. Defensively, we were very disappointing.'

Cristiano Ronaldo came on as a substitute and did save some face. His last-minute header prevented a whitewash and was United's 1,000th Premiership goal, but it provided little comfort on a Saturday night they would rather forget.

With the Chelsea game a week away and in between a tough trip to France for the Champions League return against Lille, the humiliation at the Riverside was the last thing United needed.

CHAPTER FOUR

Enough said:
Roy Keane departs as Old Trafford mourns a legend

There was only one topic of conversation as the travelling party assembled at Manchester Airport ready for the flight to Paris and the Champions League clash with Lille: Roy Keane. The Irish star may have been out of action because of the broken bone in his foot, but he was certainly not out of the headlines and one – 'Losers' – screamed out from the back of the *Mirror*. Journalists, club officials and some of the players poured over the story. According to the report, the injured skipper had been scheduled to appear on MUTV the previous evening on a regular weekly programme during which one of the squad analyses the last game.

While recording 'Roy Keane Plays the Pundit', the newspapers claimed the outspoken skipper had launched a scathing attack on several of his team-mates. Before the programme aired, it was decided by the club's hierarchy not to show it. That should have been the end of the matter, but news got out.

It was sensational stuff and some newspapers even carried quotes said to have been taken from the recording, claiming the captain had pointed a finger at some of his senior colleagues, blaming them for the recent slip in form.

The tabloids went for the jugular: 'Gagged: Reds censor Keane,' screamed the *Daily Express*. 'This lot are not up to it,' said the *Sun*, while the *Star* had the headline, 'United pull the plug on Keano.'

It was hardly the kind of send-off for an important European game and an issue Sir Alex cleverly sidestepped as he got ready for the flight. 'That is the great thing about football – we have had a few days to recover from a bad result and hopefully we can put things right tomorrow,' was his only comment.

John O'Shea added: 'Our pride was hurt on Saturday and we need to put it right for the fans and for the club. We're on top of the group and it's a great position to be in if we win.'

WEDNESDAY 2 NOVEMBER 2005

UEFA Champions League, Group Stage
Lille 1   Manchester United 0

ATTENDANCE:
65,000

UNITED: VAN DER SAR, O'SHEA, FERDINAND, BROWN, SILVESTRE, FLETCHER, SMITH, RONALDO (ROSSI 89), ROONEY, RICHARDSON (PARK 65), VAN NISTELROOY. SUBS NOT USED: HOWARD, MILLER, BARDSLEY, PIQUE, R. JONES.

After the mauling in Middlesbrough, failure in France. This major setback cast doubts on United making it through the group phase. Just when Sir Alex thought things could only get better, the manager looked on helplessly as it all went wrong in the Stade de France in Paris, where Lille were staging their home games.

Defeat came thanks to a first-half goal from former Tottenham striker Milenko Acimovic, and United almost grabbed an equaliser when Cristiano Ronaldo's header rattled the underside of the crossbar, but it was not to be. Sir Alex felt United's cause was not helped by the state of the pitch.

'One crumb of comfort is that when we face Chelsea on Sunday it will be on a better surface than that one. We tried our best and while I don't think we did enough to win, we didn't deserve to lose either. Losing matches does not help confidence that's for sure, but we can't afford to start feeling sorry for ourselves.'

Even return-again Rooney, back from his ban, could do little to crack the French resistance and the result saw Lille nudge past United into second place in a group led by the Reds' next opponents, Villarreal.

'We know the task ahead of us and if we can win our home game we can qualify,' Sir Alex added. 'The last thing we want is for it to go down to the wire with everything depending on what happens when we play Benfica in Portugal.'

Remember those words.

In the absence of Ryan Giggs and Roy Keane, it was Ruud van Nistelrooy who wore the captain's armband in France. He also aired his feelings after leading a front line that had now failed to score in three out of four Champions League games.

'Everyone goes out there and gives it their all and there is no exception in that. Now it's a matter of forgetting this, in the sense we must do things better. We wanted to bounce back and it was one defensive mistake that cost us the game. The few opportunities we had didn't really fall for us, but it was good play from them as well.'

United were not alone in defeat. Sunday's opponents Chelsea had also been rocked, although perhaps not so devastatingly. They had gone out of the Carling Cup, losing on penalties to Charlton, and consequently were not in the draw when United were given a home tie against West Bromwich Albion in round four. They also lost 1–0 to Real Betis in a Champions League game played the night before the Lille defeat, but as he prepared for the home clash with the defending champions, Sir Alex was quick to point out the difference between United and the rest.

Before the game he spoke separately to television, radio and the written press, following the same theme throughout.

It must have been a difficult week?

'It's been no tougher than any other week where you have had bad results and you have to deal with it. Of course, there's criticism from all directions and what you have to do as manager of our club is make sure the criticism remains inside your doors.'

Have United's problems deflected things away from Chelsea's failings?

'I don't think they are going to come under the same scrutiny as us. We are a fascination for everyone so that's the expectation, and I don't see anything wrong with that. We enjoy all the trappings, so we have to expect the criticism that comes along. The important thing is how we deal with criticism and the stance I take is, I don't criticise anyone in our club.

'My job is unremitting. It is unequivocal. There won't be any change. No criticism of any individual in this club and that is the example I have to set for this club. Therefore, when we deal with all this criticism, we try to keep it all indoors, we try to encourage and develop players mentally so that they can handle these situations.

'When you have young players, and when you look at the team from the other night, we had John O'Shea who is twenty-three and we had four 21-year-olds on the pitch and Wes Brown back for his first game in four months. What do you expect?

'You expect to make mistakes because young players make mistakes. They do it all the time. What helps you with experienced players is their consistency. Experienced players have been through the mill, they have been through all these tests, played-bad-and-win type of situations, but young players don't understand that you can play badly and win. They think it is all about overhead volleys and beating five men. Young players are living the dream.

'You bring it to them through experiences like Wednesday night playing on a very difficult pitch, not losing the first goal, that is to be expected. The one thing about Sunday and the same thing applies when I talk about the team at the moment, we have the ability to win. I don't think there is any doubt about that, but we know we are up against a very good team.

'They are on a fantastic run. Their consistency is terrific, therefore we are going to have to produce a top performance to win the match, helped hopefully by a support that will get behind us and keep the confidence in the team, don't let it drop, because when you lose games there is a definite dip in confidence and we are no different from anyone else in that respect.'

Can you understand what has gone wrong?

'There are a lot of reasons, reasons I don't think people are bothered to listen to, and I don't think you are bothered to listen anyway, and it doesn't make it any easier for us, simply because there is not much point discussing it, but I am operating a small squad, and we'll get on with it.

'These young lads have done fantastically because they have never deserted their post, they've all wanted to play and shown an appetite to play. They may not be as voluble as experienced players; they're a quiet team. Fine, you expect that in young players, but make no mistake about it, they have the ability and they all want to play. That is terrific and I hope they stick by that.'

Is that the key? Because they are so young no one is ready to stand up and lead from the front?

'I heard something last week that somebody said: "Wayne Rooney has got to be the leader of the team." That is all very well, you ask a twenty-year-old player to be the leader of the team. I would like to hope that is the case in terms of ability and terms of playing, yes, he leads the way in many things and not just for our club but for everybody in the game because he is a phenomenal player. But you can't expect him to lead players round about him when they are having bad spells in matches.

'Jesus Christ, the young lad's trying to sort out his own game. He's trying to progress. He wants to develop himself. He wants to be a great player. You can't expect him to go round saying, "You do your job. You do that."'

How has this week affected you personally?

'Not a bit. It doesn't bother me. It cannot bother me. If I allow it to bother me then it manifests itself right through this club.'

So it starts and stops with you?

'Of course. I'm a big boy.'

Has your own appetite remained the same?

'Yes, it has to. It hasn't diminished. I am more mellow and more assured and more considerate about things that are happening round about us, and I take my time more in terms of judging and making opinions about things, but that is what I mean about experience. That is what experience does.'

Going back to Sunday. Mourinho says he expects United to be his biggest challengers. Is that a compliment or is he just trying to wind up Arsene Wenger?

'I think he is right. We are the team who can challenge them. We have the ability, but my team will come from the players who played on Wednesday night, I've no more changes to make and, out of those twelve, Ji-sung Park has just come to the club and five are young lads, but they are all desperate to play. This morning in training they were terrific. Their attitude is good; they want to be players and there is no doubt about that.

'There are two things which will be important on Sunday: one is a good start to the game and if we get a good start the crowd will carry us the rest of the way and that will bring back the confidence of the team. We have a better surface without question; the pitch on Wednesday was an absolute joke. It is a national stadium so they have rugby, show jumping, every bloody thing on it, then you are playing a European tie.'

How do you respond to claims that there is a crisis at the club?

'We're the most famous club in the world and we have the reputation with the media that they can write anything they like about us. Sometimes it's good, don't get me wrong, sometimes it's very good, but if we have a blip then we expect a barrage.

'What you can always say about this club, and in a way it's one of the challenges of managing Manchester United, is that there is always something to attend to every day. I can be sitting here doing my work, when all of a sudden something lands on your desk that has to be attended to, sometimes in a delicate way, sometimes a positive way. You have to be patient with some things, decisive with others and that's just the nature of this job, but it's a very important aspect of it.

'This week the build-up to the game wasn't the best and it was a bad result for us, a terrible result, which puts us in a difficult position.

We have to win our next two games, and that's not the position we expected to be in. Manchester United relish these challenges. We had one last year when Arsenal came on that forty-nine game unbeaten run and, to be honest, we dominated them and hopefully we can do that on Sunday.'

The manager was forty-eight hours way from a career milestone. Sunday was the nineteenth anniversary of his appointment, but events leading up to the occasion overshadowed everything.

John O'Shea was another who was glad to see the back of what had indeed been a difficult week: 'We've experienced these times in the past and we couldn't ask for a bigger or better game to get things right. That's what we'll be looking to do. It's Chelsea at Old Trafford: they are the top team at the minute and we've got to test ourselves against them.

'The last two games have been disappointing. You go away from home and you think the teams are going to have some chances against you but, especially against Middlesbrough, it was just one of those days to forget. Now this is a perfect opportunity for everybody to liven themselves up and get a victory against Chelsea. It's still only three points, but it'll give a boost to everyone around the place.

'We've discussed a few things and we've sorted things out a bit. Today in training everybody was buzzing round, and it was great to see the energy and we've got to carry that on into the games. That's the funny thing about football. You seem to have confidence some-times and you wish you could bottle it and bring it out whenever you need it, but that is when you have to go back to the basics, working hard in training and getting things right there, then you do the simple things on the pitch. Defend properly, attack properly and eventually things will turn around.'

SUNDAY 6 NOVEMBER 2005

Barclays Premiership
Manchester United 1   Chelsea 0

SCORER:
Fletcher 31

ATTENDANCE:
67,864

UNITED: VAN DER SAR, O'SHEA, FERDINAND, BROWN, SILVESTRE, FLETCHER, SMITH, SCHOLES, ROONEY, VAN NISTELROOY (PARK 82), RONALDO. SUBS NOT USED: HOWARD, RICHARDSON, BARDSLEY, ROSSI.

Sir Alex's special day arrived, but he knew that the back-slapping and handshaking as he was congratulated on reaching nineteen years in the job would mean little if United lost. This was the big one.

Jose Mourinho rode into Old Trafford on a wave of success stretching back to Chelsea's last Premiership defeat when they had lost at Eastlands the previous season. Perhaps Manchester would prove unlucky for them again.

Every Red had their fingers crossed that would be the case and knew that what was needed was a repeat of the performance of the game against Arsenal thirteen months earlier, when the Gunners' record run was ended on an afternoon the Londoners would rather forget. Could United do it again? You bet they could!

From the start Ronaldo was a constant threat creating the first scoring attempt after beating Ferreira. Chelsea responded. Didier Drogba tried to force home a Frank Lampard pass, but his effort was saved by Edwin van der Sar. Wayne Rooney chased a Silvestre pass and picked out Scholes on the edge of the box, but he shot the wrong side of the post.

Half an hour had gone when Ronaldo sent Del Horno the wrong way before crossing deep to the far post. Darren Fletcher ran in and headed firmly across goal. The ball flew over John Terry and Petr Cech and into the net. Old Trafford erupted.

'There are people who said I didn't intend to score, that I was heading across goal, but to be honest it was a bit of both. I intended the ball to go back over the goalkeeper towards the back post, with either somebody coming in and scoring or it going into the net.

'Luckily it went in, but there was no intention one way or another.

I just thought to myself, "play the percentages." I wanted to get it back over the goalkeeper into the right area so that if Ruud or one of the strikers was coming in it was just an easy tap-in, and if it goes in itself then great,' is Darren's recollection of the magical moment.

'Amazingly you do have time to think even in that split second, but most of the time it is just the percentage. Your thoughts are: "Am I going to be able to do anything here, if I can get this up high and over the 'keeper towards the back post. There are no players to my left to knock it down to, the goalkeeper's coming out towards me. The defenders are coming too."

'It was the only way it was possible for us to get a goal in that situation and yes, you do think. Whether it is split-second instinct or what I don't know, but things like that happen.'

Chelsea sought a swift equaliser. Drogba, Lampard and Joe Cole were a threat. United almost got a second in the fifty-fourth minute, but van Nistelrooy's shot flew over the bar. Drogba came close to scoring while lying on the ground, but O'Shea's determination kept him out, not once but twice. The strain showed on both teams and referee Graham Poll had his hands full, booking Drogba, Ferreira, Gallas, Makelele, Smith, Ronaldo and Fletcher.

With seven minutes left, Rooney went close after Ji-sung Park won the ball on the edge of the Chelsea box, but that was United's last clear-cut chance and from then to the end, they were forced to defend against a barrage of attacks from the London side. Like Arsenal before them, their long run had ended at Old Trafford, but at least Sir Alex could sip a celebratory glass in peace that evening and look back, not perhaps on the end of a troublesome week, but on nineteen years of achievement at Old Trafford.

The fourth senior goal of Darren Fletcher's career had lifted a huge weight off everyone at Old Trafford.

'It was nice to have scored it, but it was just great to get the win for the team. There was a lot of criticism in the week; different things happened in the club and we had the bad result in Europe. I think the chips were down a little bit, so for everybody, the players and the staff, everyone around the club and the fans obviously, it was an important goal because we won the match.

'It's definitely the most important goal I have scored for United. I scored for Scotland at Hampden that took us to the play-offs after I had come off the bench for the first time. That was important, but to score against Chelsea and end that great undefeated run was significant.

'It was important for the players, everyone, not just me. Obviously scoring a goal was nice, but the most crucial thing was we beat Chelsea, that the team won. Me scoring is irrelevant, the whole club needed that victory. Because of the circumstances in the build-up to the game nobody fancied us, everybody thought we were going to get beat, but we pulled out a good result.'

The thirteen-day gap before the next game, as yet another international break loomed, gave Sir Alex an opportunity to turn his attention to other matters, among them the completion of Cristiano Ronaldo's contract negotiations, and he joined Kieran Richardson and Phil Bardsley as the latest of the young ones to extend their stay at the club.

On Friday 18 November, before discussing the trip to Charlton, the manager made his feelings known: 'We're delighted. It's taken a bit of time and it got a bit frustrating, but you have to remember that his agent and his lawyer are over in Portugal and it's never easy to get the parties together a lot of the time. Now the job's been done. The contract was completed this morning and he's signed and it represents our hopes for the future in terms of building a young side again. All the young players are under long contracts now which is good news and we will now see young Ronaldo develop into the world-class player we know he is going to be.'

There were also improvements on the injury front. Wes Brown was playing again and Gary Neville was close to a comeback after an hour run-out in the reserves.

'He'll travel with us tomorrow. Unfortunately, Ryan Giggs has been to see the specialist who says he won't be able to start training for another two weeks, but it is better being careful after an injury like that. Other than that, there is no other news.'

Carrington had again been a lonely place for the manager.

'Aye, that is definitely a frustrating thing. It really is. Only Scholesy and Silvestre were in during the week. John O'Shea came in on Thursday because the Republic didn't have a game and he had been back to Ireland for a few days' break. There was no real coming together of the players after the Chelsea game, which is important because you could have got feedback from them. You could have got a sense of exhilaration in their manner in the dressing room but we lost that because of the internationals. We hope we get it back.'

The break had taken Ji-sung Park to the other side of the world and the manager was waiting for him to check back and there was also an injury scare surrounding Ruud van Nistelrooy. He had been withdrawn from the Holland squad, but Sir Alex cleared any doubts over his fitness.

'He's OK. One hundred per cent. We have to thank Holland for being professional about it; they respected Ruud's position and also our position and I think that's good.'

It seemed a fairly routine day. The manager went through his usual string of press conferences without the slightest hint that a massive story was about to break. Rumours were circulating in Ireland. A radio station in Cork had broken what would be a sensational story if it turned out to be true. By the time it filtered through to reach Carrington, the media circus had dispersed.

'We heard the Irish newspapers had got hold of it that morning. Somehow it leaked out that way and that sped up the press release,' Sir Alex later revealed.

The statement, published on the club's official website caused a knee-jerk reaction across the football world.

'Manchester United have reached an agreement with Roy Keane which allows him to leave the club with immediate effect. The agreement enables Keane to sign a long-term deal with another club and secure his playing career beyond what would have been the end of his contract at United in the summer.

'The club has offered Roy a testimonial in recognition of his twelve and a half years at Old Trafford and thanks Roy for his major contribution to the club during his years of service.

'It has been a great honour and privilege for me to play for Manchester United for over twelve years,' said Keane in a statement. 'During my time at the club, I have been fortunate to play alongside some of the best players in the game and in front of the best supporters in the world. At all times I have endeavoured to do my best for the management and the team.

'While it is a sad day for me to leave such a great club and manager, I believe that the time has now come for me to move on. After so many years, I will miss everyone at the club. I send my best wishes for the future to the management, players, staff and supporters of the club,' he added.

United boss Sir Alex Ferguson described Keane as the best midfielder of his generation. 'Roy has been a fantastic servant for Manchester United,' said Sir Alex. 'The best midfield player in the world of his generation, he is already one of the great figures in our club's illustrious history. Roy has been central to the success of the club in the last twelve and a half years, and everyone at Old Trafford wishes him well in the rest of his career and beyond.'

Chief executive David Gill added: 'Roy has been a towering figure at the club for over a decade. His dedication, talent and leadership have been qualities that have marked him out as one of the true greats. On behalf of everyone at the club, we wish him every success in his future career.'

The following morning, Roy Keane's name filled every back page.

He figured prominently in every news broadcast for the next twenty-four hours, but at the team's London hotel, Sir Alex had to concentrate on the task ahead: the clash with Charlton.

This was a huge game. Firstly, United had to show the world life would go on without Roy Keane, but more importantly they had to make sure the win over Chelsea was not wasted. The manager needed no reminding that a year earlier after ending Arsenal's long unbeaten run, United had lost to Portsmouth at Fratton Park.

'It's a significant comment that, because after that victory against Arsenal, we thought we were on a run. The confidence was back, but a great performance was followed by a disappointing game at Portsmouth, a game we should have won by maybe five or six. But we didn't. We lost. Now we have a similar situation. We go to Charlton after a great result against Chelsea and I would be bitterly disappointed if we didn't get a victory tomorrow.'

SATURDAY 20 NOVEMBER 2005

SOCRERS:
Smith 37,
Van Nistelrooy 70,
85

ATTENDANCE:
26,730

Barclays Premiership
Charlton Athletic 1   Manchester United 3

UNITED: VAN DER SAR, BROWN, FERDINAND, SILVESTRE, O'SHEA, FLETCHER (BARDSLEY 89), SMITH, SCHOLES, RONALDO (PARK 75), ROONEY, VAN NISTELROOY (RICHARDSON 85). SUBS NOT USED: HOWARD, ROSSI.

After the drama of the previous twenty-four hours, it was hardly surprising Roy Keane was uppermost in the minds of the United supporters who gathered at The Valley. Passionate choruses of 'Keano, Keano!' rang from the ranks of the travelling army throughout the game. His departure was the only topic of conversation on the journey to south London and anyone not ready to air an opinion simply stared in disbelief at the selection of speculative stories that filled the back pages.

Many claimed Keane's outspoken comments in that MUTV interview had been the final straw. The guessing game had started. Where next for Keane? Was he being lined up for the vacant Ireland job? Would he return as manager when Sir Alex retires?

Anyone worried that the situation would affect the team's performance quickly had their answer. United tore into Charlton and set up a string of chances with Wayne Rooney, Ruud van Nistelrooy and Cristiano Ronaldo in fine form, but half time was approaching before they finally scored.

Charlton had just had their best attack when United broke. Ronaldo, John O'Shea and Darren Fletcher inter-passed before Alan

Smith – the man filling Keane's place – fired home from the edge of the box.

The second half began with United looking for a second, but it was Charlton who scored next as Darren Ambrose hit home a powerful drive. Their joy lasted five minutes. Rooney laid on the pass which set up van Nistelrooy to make it 2–1 and the Dutchman did it again shortly before the end to tie things up.

Sir Alex had got his wish. 'After the great performance against Chelsea, we could not afford anything other than a win. Let's hope it starts us on a good run. If we maintain that same hunger and desire, we will be hard to beat.'

This was the first time he had spoken since the club made the announcement about Keane and he told MUTV: 'I was pleased the fans paid their tribute to Roy the way they did because, as you know, he is one of the greatest players in the history of our club and certainly the best in my time.

'The influence he had on the team over a ten-year spell was enormous. Now we move on to Tuesday, which is our most important game of the past few years. Our ambitions to do well in Europe are always there and we have to win this game to have any chance of qualifying for the next stage.'

While Sir Alex concentrated on Villarreal, for the players it was time to contemplate life without the man who had walked away the previous day. Ruud van Nistelrooy was obviously affected and seemed close to tears: 'It's a difficult time. We only heard the news about Roy yesterday after training and it was all so quick and so intense. That news was just a big shock. We had to just forget about it for a little while to play the game and try to deal with it again from now on.

'For me he's been the most influential man who's been around in my career. I am in the fortunate position to say that I worked with him for four and a half years and it's amazing how much you can learn, and I think I have done that. But it is still a sad day. He's so loved by the players. Obviously he's been the captain for such a long time and led us out and he was always there, for the team and for the club and for the people who worked at Carrington or Old Trafford or with the kids. He knew everything about the club.

'He is a real man with a big heart for United and I think that spirit can continue. That's what we need to make sure. You can't compare him with anything else and that is why it was difficult for me.

'It was a big shock and sort of a sad day as well, but I think the fans were lovely today. They were unbelievable, supporting the manager, supporting Roy and supporting us, which I think was the collective feeling of us today. Sometimes it's difficult when big moments like this happen. We could never foresee this. They all say life goes on, and it does in the end, but still you have to deal with this.'

Apart from the official announcement, United and Roy maintained their silence in the days that followed, but eventually Sir Alex explained the events of 18 November.

'David Gill and I had agreed with Roy and his lawyer the deal for him to leave and what he wanted before he left and it was done the right way. We conducted the release that morning. Roy hadn't been training. I went in and told the players at the end of the training session and I knew quite a lot of them would be shocked, but as we said at the time, we parted on good terms. We shook hands Roy and I, and he knows that everything I do and everything that I have ever done is for Manchester United, and he was the same.

'He has been in to see me since then and we have had a good chat and there is absolutely no animosity. He was a great, great player for me, but it is just one of these situations: it was the right time for him.'

Gary Neville will never forget the moment he found out: 'I wasn't training that day and Ronaldo, Quinton and I were pulled by the manager in the car park because the other players were out on the training pitch. The manager just said that he had something to say. I knew obviously, because I was injured together with Roy for about two months. I was with him every day.

'I was just disappointed really that Roy had to leave the club, because he was a great example to all the players, somebody who I personally learned a lot from. It was just a really disappointing day for everybody: for the manager, for Roy, for the players. You have some shocks in football, but that was a big shock.'

'I think everyone was shocked,' was the Ryan Giggs view. 'When a player leaves, especially in the middle of the season, it is always a shock and someone of the stature of Keaney who has been such a great player, a great leader, a great captain. It was a big shock to everyone because when players have been there for so long you want them to carry on.

'Keaney moved on, he felt it was the right time, but you have just got to be professional about it and get on with your job. You may be friends with them or be really close to them, but you have just got to concentrate on playing football. In Roy we have lost a lot: our leader, our captain, such an influential player. You lose so much, but the thing about Manchester United is you may lose great players, but the team always goes on.

'We have lost other players in recent years, the likes of Schmeichel, Cantona, Beckham, but the team goes on and it always will. That is what is great about Man United; thirty or forty years ago you saw Charlton, Best, Law, but you lose them and you have just got to get on with it and rebuild another team.

'My lasting memory of Roy is simply someone who you would always want in your team. If you were picking a team, Keaney's would be the first name on the sheet and it is as simple as that. Even if he was playing below par he would just get that much more out of the players around him. It didn't really depend on his performance, even though his performances were rarely bad, but if they were he would just get that bit more out of the people around him and that sets him apart from the other great players who have been in the team.'

For Waterford born John O'Shea, it was farewell to a boyhood hero.

'It was quite a wrench for me losing somebody like that; someone who had always been around. When I came into the club, to have him as the captain was just a great feeling, to know you had an Irishman there in your corner.

'When I got into the team he was there to fight your corner for you with referees or other players, with everybody. To know that he was there to back you up, but he didn't just do it for me, he did it for anyone who was playing in the XI with him. You could see the way he dragged us through some games at times and he did that for Ireland, too. I was fortunate enough to be able to play with him in the Irish team and there are some memories I will always cherish. He was a hero without a doubt because of what he was able to do.

'It looked as if he was going to miss the boat when he was a youngster, not getting a chance to play in England, but he kept plugging away and joined a soccer scheme. He was fortunate enough to get a trial over at Nottingham Forest and virtually took England by storm in the next three or four years. That was an amazing achievement and he carried it on to the next level.

'Life has to go on without him and that is one of the first things the manager said. He told us we have lost probably one of the best players he had ever had at the club, but we had to make sure we got over it as quickly as we could.'

As a fellow midfielder, Darren Fletcher had added reason to admire Keane: 'He was a massive influence on me since I came to the club and well before I was in the first team. You get told at a young age to watch players who play in your position and I had the privilege of watching Roy, Paul Scholes, Seba Veron, Nicky Butt, and trying to take bits of their games.

'I think Roy's actual game didn't get appreciated enough, because people saw him as the leader, the captain. His first touch, his range of passing, everything about his game was immaculate. Those were the things I looked at and, while his leadership qualities were second to none and his influence was massive on all the players, I like to remember him as the great player he was.

'I thought he was a world-class football player and he could drive the team forward, was an inspirational captain and a role model for everyone. But life had to go on.'

Gary Neville added: 'I rang him up and wished him all the best and, to be honest, Roy isn't one for pleasantries and I said that to him on the phone. But I did wish him all the best and was really sorry about what had happened, and I genuinely was.

'I had been injured with him for six weeks before that and being in the presence of Roy, training with him every day, he is a challenge. Roy is a challenge to everybody in the sense that he will challenge you to get the best out of you all the time. He will question you all the time. Some people could see that as a negative, but I always saw it as a positive because he questioned, "Are you doing enough? Are you actually giving your all? Are you performing well enough?" Even if you were giving your all, was it still good enough? Always challenging you. That is something to me that, with him leaving, I will miss. He had that special aura about him.'

The players had little time to dwell on events of the weekend as they checked in for training on the Monday of what was to prove another eventful week at the club, but for very different reasons.

The following day United faced Villarreal in the Champions League, but news coming from London overshadowed the build-up. Seven weeks after George Best had been admitted to hospital, his condition had deteriorated badly. The player who had captured the hearts of millions during the sixties was fighting for his life. Reports on his condition made it clear that those years battling alcoholism, which eventually led to a liver transplant, had taken their toll, and there were strong fears that he would not survive this latest setback.

Sir Alex faced a battery of television cameras when he stepped onto the rostrum for the pre-match press conference. He and Edwin van der Sar posed momentarily for still shots before getting down to business, with the manager brusquely fending off the first question.

'Sir Alex, a difficult few days and millions of Manchester United fans will be wondering, where does the club go now without Roy Keane?'

Sir Alex was in no mood to expand on what had already been said.

'Is that part of the Villarreal game? We've a big game tomorrow and it's important our concentration is on the game itself because we realise it's such a vital game for the club. Over the years we have been very good in the group stage. We have always had good home form and we have got to rely on that now, because winning tomorrow would put us in a much stronger position than we are in at the moment.'

He was willing to discuss who would succeed Keane as captain, albeit for the short term.

'We've had a fantastic response from Ruud van Nistelrooy, absolutely brilliant, and Paul Scholes was quite happy someone else should have the armband. I don't think he was enjoying being captain. So at the moment I'm delighted at the experience Ruud has, the manner of him, his demeanour is excellent, his professionalism. Everything is right and we are getting a great response. Obviously when Gary and Ryan come back I have a decision to make, but I don't think it's monumental. The more important issue at this time is to make sure we win games, create the atmosphere we had on Saturday, and against Chelsea. Fantastic.'

Asked if there was a player within the current squad likely to follow in the footsteps of the great captains he had appointed during his time in charge – Bryan Robson, Steve Bruce, Eric Cantona, Roy Keane – Sir Alex replied: 'Ruud is doing the job very well at the moment and Ryan has had the armband many times when Roy wasn't available purely on seniority. I think that is quite right, a player who has served the length of time that Ryan Giggs has at this football club deserves to be recognised. He has great respect. He is a wonderful professional.

'Then you have Gary Neville who, just like Ryan, has served his time here. He's a loyal man. He's a very enthusiastic and emotional person. Different qualities. Who is to say that from one of those three we couldn't make a captain? There are other examples in the club who desire maybe to be captain, like Alan Smith and Wayne Rooney. They would love to be captain – that's what Wayne's always telling me anyway! Nonetheless, it's not a monumental decision at this moment in time. Tomorrow Ruud van Nistelrooy will be captain.'

TUESDAY 22 NOVEMBER 2005

UEFA Champions League, Group Stage
Manchester United 0   Villarreal 0

ATTENDANCE:
67,471

UNITED: VAN DER SAR, BROWN (NEVILLE 73), FERDINAND, SILVESTRE, O'SHEA,
FLETCHER (PARK 53), SMITH (SAHA 81), SCHOLES, RONALDO, ROONEY, VAN NISTELROOY.
SUBS NOT USED: HOWARD, RICHARDSON, PIQUE, ROSSI.

'Massive' is an overworked adjective in football speak, but not this time. United were a step away from the Last Chance Saloon. They had to beat the Spaniards or face the prospect of a must-win closing game against Benfica in Portugal.

'It's massive now for us,' said Sir Alex before kick-off. 'The key is to really get the fans going. They were great, and they helped us through that thing about losing the two games. They just picked everybody up. When Old Trafford's like that there is no place in Britain to match it.'

The message hit home. A wall of sound greeted the teams for the first post-Keane home game. There had been an early boost when Villarreal arrived in Manchester without both their main goal-scorers, Diego Forlan and Juan Riquelme, and, not surprisingly, they took a negative approach, spreading men across midfield, but while the visitors had good reason for their lack of bite, United had no excuse, as the goals dried up again.

With van Nistelrooy, Rooney, Smith, Scholes and Ronaldo in the side, there was plenty of ability up front, but even after Saha and Park were brought from the bench, no one could produce the goal to put United through to the knock-out phase.

It was not to be. The most crucial game so far in the campaign ended goalless. The dream of a third European Cup was fading. The one glimmer of hope came from the section's other game between Lille and Benfica, which had also ended all square. United could qualify by beating Benfica, or a draw in Lisbon would be good enough provided Villarreal won their final home game against Lille.

'These things happen in life. It's an open group now and all the teams have to win in their last games,' said a philosophical Sir Alex.

The stand-in skipper shared the manager's viewpoint: 'We were looking for a win here today, that was our goal, but we didn't succeed. We did well in the first half, but the pity was we couldn't do the same in the second, otherwise I am sure we would have had a bigger chance to win. We had a few chances, not all clear-cut, but a couple were and we had some good spells of play which at times were excellent. In the second half they did things differently in midfield and we found it harder to cope with. Qualification is at least in our own hands, but we know we will have to perform to get through,' said van Nistelrooy.

'It was a fairly decent performance, but in the final third we lacked a bit of composure and perhaps the rub of the green,' was the Rio Ferdinand assessment. 'But it tells the story so far in the Champions League campaign; teams have come to Old Trafford and tried to stifle us and they managed to do that today. No side in this group has scored many goals and that tells us that everyone has gone to away grounds and just tried to keep solid and remain goalless. I suppose we'd rather be in this position, where we know what we've got to do, rather than waiting for other results to come in and relying on other teams. We have to rely on our own performance and our own result.'

For Rio a big weekend loomed. United were away to his former club West Ham, where his younger brother Anton now played in the position he had occupied during his days at Upton Park.

'It's a game all the family will be looking forward to and the kind of occasion you won't be able to take in at the time, but afterwards you will and, fingers crossed, we get the three points. I will approach it like any other game, there's a ball to be won and you've got to win it. Obviously he's my brother, but on the pitch I'll be playing for Man United and looking to do everything I can to get a win,' he added.

The players would travel down to London on Saturday 26 November, but twenty-four hours before that, the manager had his usual interview demands to fulfil. He confessed to having mixed feelings about Upton Park: 'We have lost two league titles there. We lost 1–0 the year we had to play the four games in six days, and the next time? How we drew I will never know. We did and we lost the league. It was an amazing game when we could have scored twenty! I will always remember the right-back, Tim Breaker, flicked the ball away with his hand and everybody saw it but the referee. Those two memories are not great, but on the whole our record has been OK down there.'

He also confirmed that he had lost interest in Michael Ballack. He categorically denied claims he was in line to take over at Rangers.

'I was embarrassed by that story. The *Sun* must have known I was going to Scotland to open an old age home and, of course, they asked me the question: "Am I going to Rangers?" It is so embarrassing and poor bloody Alex McLeish is struggling for his job.'

He again cleared up doubts about his future: 'What I said was "when I am finished with United, I am finished" and that is exactly right. What you don't have knowledge of is your health. I am feeling great now. I feel terrific, but obviously I am not going to be here for ten years, I don't think I will be here in four years.

'I am just flying off the top of my head, but I have absolutely no idea when the day will come, because we have never set anything. We agreed that with the club two or three years ago, "Let's not talk about retirement because it just becomes a problem." A mindset comes in and I am not going down that road. It is not on the agenda. Definitely not. Not even a thought about it.'

He admitted he was looking forward to meeting up with one of the Manchester United 'family' the next day. Teddy Sheringham was enjoying the autumn of his playing days with the Hammers, having filled a leading role in the most successful period of United's history. He had left Old Trafford in 2001 to move to former club Tottenham Hotspur before switching to West Ham where he had helped them win promotion in 2004–05.

'It's amazing. Fantastic. I spoke to him a little while ago and what is he? Thirty-nine years old, forty in March? Jeez. It's amazing.'

The final interview had just finished when Sir Alex learned the United family had lost one of its favourite sons.

At 12.55 p.m. on Friday 25 November 2005, George Best died.

The news was broken to reporters waiting outside the London hospital.

'After a long and very valiant fight, Mr George Best died this afternoon in the intensive care unit at Cromwell Hospital.'

Tributes poured in. Denis Law had spent Thursday evening at George's bedside: 'From 1964 to 1969 he was the best player in the country. It's sad as hell, but I don't think we saw the best of him. He went on the blink at a time when he could have got even better.'

Sir Bobby Charlton, who like Law had played alongside Best at his peak, reflected: 'He was on a par, at least, with anyone you can name. We at Manchester United have learned from our experience with George. With Eric Cantona, we had to treat him differently, make allowances. If instead of being hostile to George, which I was, we had leaned a bit and tried to help him, who knows?'

Sir Alex: 'At this moment in time I just keep thinking of him as a player because these are the moments we are going to relish when we think of George Best. My particular memory of him is when he played against Scotland at Windsor Park and he tore them apart. Tommy Gemmell of Celtic was marking him and he was a great full-back of his time, but George gave him a mother and father of a doing. What I thought was astonishing that day was George was back tackling Tommy and then sprinting up the pitch to attack. He was just a phenomenal player.

'Some people are born to their craft like that. He had amazing courage. You have seen pictures of him with his socks around his ankles taking kicks from guys like Ron Harris and Norman Hunter and Tommy Smith. They were serious guys, but he came through all that and every time he got fouled he got up and said "give me the ball".

'There'll be a million memories, and all good ones.'

SUNDAY 27 NOVEMBER 2005

Barclays Premiership
West Ham United 1   Manchester United 2

UNITED: VAN DER SAR, BROWN, FERDINAND, SILVESTRE (NEVILLE 37), O'SHEA, FLETCHER, SMITH, SCHOLES, PARK, ROONEY, VAN NISTELROOY (RICHARDSON 90). SUBS NOT USED: HOWARD, RONALDO, SAHA.

SCORERS:
Rooney 47,
O'Shea 55

ATTENDANCE:
34,755

Many of the 34,000-plus crowd gathered inside Upton Park never saw George Best play but all knew of his fame. They had seen black and white images of 'Genius George' mesmerising Benfica's defenders in the 1968 European Cup final as the story of the wonder boy of British football was told on every news bulletin. Some even knew it was on this ground he had played a leading role in a 6–1 massacre, as United clinched the title in 1967. George scored United's fourth during an amazing first half, so it was fitting that West Ham officials should choose to mark his death with applause rather than with the traditional minute's silence.

Speeches from Sir Bobby Charlton and Sir Trevor Brooking preceded the gesture, which lifted the solemnity of the occasion and United fans made their own moving contribution by chanting George Best's name not only during the minute of applause, but throughout the whole of the game. It was something George would have appreciated, but not perhaps what followed the kick off.

Within sixty seconds, United were a goal down as Marlon Harewood scored. The Reds re-grouped and went at West Ham, who included two former Old Trafford stars in their starting line-up: not only Teddy Sheringham but also Roy Carroll, who had left in the summer as Edwin van der Sar arrived. His former team-mates made sure he had a busy afternoon.

United had chances during the first forty-five minutes, but the second half was three minutes old before they equalised. Ji-sung Park started the move and found Rooney, whose shot on the run beat the diving Carroll.

The goal lifted United. They tore into the West Ham half and, eight minutes later, their efforts paid off as Scholes took a corner on the right, John O'Shea met it perfectly and his header tied up the win. United had turned things round to step into second place ahead of Arsenal, but they were still ten points adrift of Chelsea.

Back in Manchester, something quite remarkable was happening. Since Friday, fans in their droves had been arriving at Old Trafford to leave flowers, photographs, scarves, replica shirts, every kind of football memorabilia imaginable. A giant shrine had grown in Sir Matt Busby Way made from hundreds of scarves, thousands of flowers and millions of memories.

The collection grew by the hour, and over the weekend had been transformed into a giant crocodile of colour that sprawled along the pavement opposite Old Trafford's frontage. Hundreds turned up to leave their token, thousands more to see the spectacle. Supporters stood in silence, reading the messages of condolence, some photographing the scene for those unable to make the pilgrimage. Many tried to hold back the tears, others wept openly. Life had to go on and it was here that fate played its part.

George Best had made his Manchester United debut as a seventeen-year-old on 14 September 1963 in a league game against West Bromwich Albion. Forty-two years on, and in the first game after his death, United were due to face Albion once more, this time in the fourth round of the Carling Cup.

Small consolation. Cristiano Ronaldo heads in United's 1000th Premiership goal at the Riverside, but Boro had already scored four in United's worst defeat of the season.

Despite a heroic performance from Edwin van der Sar against Lille, things did not get any better as Acimovic's goal dropped United out of the qualifying positions in their Champions League group.

Darren Fletcher celebrates scoring the winning goal against Chelsea in November. After all the criticism the team had been facing, this result was one of the most important of the season.

Watching in the stands for the last time as a United player, Roy Keane would leave the club within a fortnight. In over twelve years at the club, he had been one of the greatest players ever to pull on the red shirt.

Mikael Silvestre wins his header against Didier Drogba, as United's rearguard holds firm.

Alan Smith scores his only goal of the season to help United on their way to a 3–1 victory over Charlton in the first game of the post-Keane era.

Rio and Anton Ferdinand congratulate each other at the end of United's 2–1 victory over West Ham. Elder brother Rio was also to win the battle to score most goals in the season.

Above: Just one of the tributes to United legend George Best, who died on 25 November. He was a player that football fans everywhere loved and admired.

Above right: Sir Alex Ferguson and ex-United captain Bryan Robson lead out the teams ahead of United's Carling Cup tie against West Brom. It was an emotional evening at Old Trafford, beginning with a minute's silence while the crowd held up pictures of Best.

Louis Saha had mixed emotions: it was his first start since April, and he scored with a twenty-yard drive, but his thoughts were with Best.

Paul Scholes scores his first goal since May as he heads home a Giggs corner to set United on the way to a 3–0 victory over Portsmouth at the beginning of a hectic December.

Cristiano Ronaldo is substituted during United's shock defeat at Benfica that dumped them out of the Champions League.

After three and a half years and on his 140th appearance, Rio Ferdinand rises above the Wigan defence to head home.

Wayne Rooney scores the second goal against Aston Villa early in the second half to ensure United went into the Christmas period on a high.

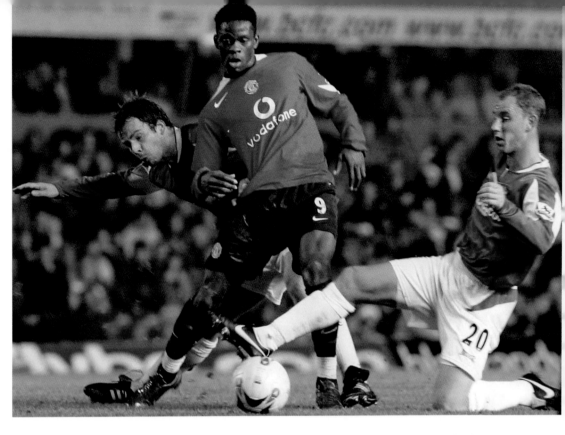

Louis Saha was again on target in the Carling Cup as he scored two in United's 3–1 quarter-final victory over Birmingham. Here former Red Nicky Butt does his best to stop him.

Ruud van Nistelrooy was on target again to help United to a comfortable 3–0 victory over West Brom in the league; United had taken twenty-two points out of the last twenty-four, but still trailed Chelsea by nine.

CHAPTER FIVE

Farewell George, goodbye Europe

The ceremony that preceded the West Brom cup-tie at Old Trafford was both moving and magnificent. Understandably, there was a sombre atmosphere as spectators assembled in the stadium. Manchester United was mourning the loss of one of its most famous sons, so the build-up to the game began quietly, even with 48,294 present. Many came to say farewell to George Best and their presence gave what, under normal circumstances, would have been regarded by most as a mediocre game, an attendance that many clubs would covet.

Possibly because West Brom were managed by former Old Trafford hero Bryan Robson, probably because everyone present realised the importance of the occasion, supporters from both clubs behaved impeccably during the short pre-match tribute. With the teams forming a guard of honour, Bryan Robson and Sir Alex laid wreaths alongside a banner made by United fans that read: 'George – Simply the Best', the penultimate act of a ceremony that began as players past and present were introduced by veteran journalist David Meek, former United correspondent of the *Manchester Evening News*.

Calum Best, George's twenty-four-year-old son, led out the procession, which included members of the 1968 European Cup side and the 1963 West Brom side, among them full-back Graham Williams, the man who had been given the task of marking the teenage debutant. According to George's close pal Paddy Crerand, Williams left

Old Trafford afterwards suffering from 'twisted blood', but could lay claim to being the first of a long list of opponents who had been bamboozled by the Irish Imp's skills.

Sir Bobby Charlton told the crowd: 'I would just like to pay my respects like everyone who is here, to George Best, who was a giant in the game of football. On behalf of all of the Manchester United family here in the stadium, the players, the staff and indeed all the Manchester United fans around the world, I would just like to say a big thank you to George Best. You will never be forgotten here.'

Then came one of Old Trafford's most emotional moments. Each spectator had been given a poster bearing a giant picture of George. On the signal to start a one-minute silence given by the referee's whistle everyone, including those visiting fans whose behaviour was a credit to Albion, was asked to hold their poster aloft. George was here, there and everywhere – as if he was playing again.

WEDNESDAY 30 NOVEMBER 2005

SCORERS:
Ronaldo 11 (pen),
Saha 16,
O'Shea 56

ATTENDANCE:
48,294

Carling Cup, Fourth Round
Manchester United 3   West Bromwich Albion 1

UNITED: HOWARD, NEVILLE, FERDINAND, SILVESTRE, RICHARDSON, FLETCHER (R. JONES 59), O'SHEA (PIQUE 67), PARK (BARDSLEY 63), RONALDO, SAHA, ROSSI. SUBS NOT USED: ROONEY, STEELE.

According to Sir Alex, this was one match United could not afford to lose. The declaration had nothing to do with any aspirations of adding the Carling Cup to his trophy collection, or maintaining the current four-game unbeaten run. It was all about George Best.

'I knew West Brom would be playing a strong side and I wanted to win tonight because, on this occasion, I didn't want anything about the evening to be flat. That is why I also played a strong side,' he said, after making eight changes to the starting line-up fielded against Barnet in the previous round.

Gary Neville returned for his first start since August, joining Rio Ferdinand and Mikael Silvestre in a back four completed by Kieran

Richardson. Cristiano Ronaldo, John O'Shea, Ji-sung Park and Darren Fletcher created a solid midfield with Giuseppe Rossi and Louis Saha, also back from injury, leading the attack.

From the off, United's intentions were abundantly clear. A sixth-minute Saha strike was ruled out for offside but, five minutes later, they did score when Ronaldo made no mistake from the penalty spot after being brought down by Diomansy Kamara. Next into the spot-light was the teenage Rossi. He played the perfect pass into Saha's path and the Frenchman's low shot squirmed under the body of Albion 'keeper Russell Hoult. Two–nil.

The third came ten seconds into the second half, with John O'Shea scoring after an impressive one-two with Saha. United were cruising and the home support spent the last twenty minutes singing songs of past heroes Solskjaer, Cantona and Keane capped by a rousing, 'We all live in a Georgie Best world.'

Even an Albion goal headed home by Nathan Ellington in the seventy-seventh minute had little effect. Nothing could stop United winning on a night made for memories.

Scorer O'Shea was among those moved by the occasion. 'I will always remember all those fans holding up the picture of George during the minute's silence, then the minute's celebration. It really was an amazing feeling to be part of it and to remember such a fan-tastic talent. It was definitely lump-in-the-throat time, and the hairs on the back of your neck were standing up.

'Obviously all of the team and probably many of the fans didn't see George play, so we had been watching all the clips on television of his goals and the things he had done and you soon realised he was one of the best players in the world.

'My goal wasn't a bad move to be fair. I picked it up in midfield and was able to play a ball in to Louis and he went for the one-two and was able to get it back in over the defender and I finished it with a volley into the net, so it was a nice goal because they don't come around too often. I really enjoyed that one, especially on the occasion that it was.'

For Louis Saha there were mixed emotions. Joy, because it was his first start since April, had to subdued by the solemnity of the pre-match ritual.

'The feeling was big. But every time you have a feeling like that you have to be aware that it is not the important thing. You have to make sure you play a professional game and that is what I try to do every time. I did feel something special. It was so huge for the club and so huge for any person, not only from United, but also for those who knew the quality of George Best. It is a great shame he has gone, but he left some good memories behind, so that is the main concern. If you are a man and you left no trace in your life, no kids or whatever, it would be a shame. He did a good job.

'I have to admit my father knew more about him than me, but it is enough just looking at the eyes of people when they say his name, so it is an amazing feeling to be at the same club where he did so many magical things. It was very emotional. I won't say it was difficult, but very emotional.'

Ryan Giggs watched the game from the main stand and possibly felt closer to George than some of the other players.

'It affected everyone around the club, but I was lucky enough to work on a video with George after I had been in the first team for two or three years. I spent a couple of days filming with him around Manchester and down at The Cliff and around the town. It was a great experience for me to be with someone who was obviously such a great player.

'You could see how much respect the fans had for him, chanting his name and cheering. He was one of a kind, really. He was the first superstar footballer, but more than that, he was world class. Even though I was unfortunate not to see him play or to see that many video clips of him, what I have seen is the great balance, vision and bravery that everyone talked about.'

There was added reason for Ryan to feel close to George. Had he not been burdened with the tag 'the new George Best' when he broke into the first team in 1991?

'It never really bothered me. It was something I always took as a compliment. To be compared to such a great player that is all I could do. I remember first seeing it in the paper when I was about sixteen and it referred to me as "the next George Best". I wondered what was happening, because I had never been compared to anyone before. I had my own style of playing, but to find yourself compared to such a great player told me I must be doing something right!'

Sir Alex felt pride in what he had witnessed before and during the game: 'The club organised it in a special way and throughout the night the fans made it as fitting a tribute to George as they possibly could. I say well done to them for that. It was very moving before the game. Wonderful! I spoke to young Calum before the kick-off and he was so delighted at the reception and we are all pleased it has gone off so well.

'I was absolutely delighted to see Louis Saha back on the score-sheet again. When you see how he played tonight, you see what a great striker he is. He is going to be a great addition to us and we all hope and pray he now stays clear of injuries and we can add that potent striker to the forces we have with Wayne Rooney, Ruud van Nistelrooy, Ji-sung Park, Cristiano Ronaldo and young Rossi. It gives us a great armoury for the big month ahead.'

One of his duties in that 'big month' was to attend George Best's funeral in Belfast. It was held on Saturday 3 December, the morning of United's 5.15 p.m. clash with Portsmouth and meant that the manager faced a testing schedule to be present at both events.

'The Ulster police have organised things very well, so hopefully it will go without any hiccups. It gives us an opportunity to meet George's family and it will be a very emotional day over there. You can just imagine what it is going to be like. There will be thousands and thousands there. Then it's a rush back to Old Trafford for the game, which is an important match for us.'

He was right. United lay second in the Premiership, a point ahead of Arsenal but ten adrift of leaders Chelsea. To stand any chance of closing the gap, they had to keep winning and hope the defending champions would slip.

Ole Gunnar Solskjaer represented the present-day players and made the trip to Belfast with Sir Alex for a funeral shown live on television around the world and which was seen as a fitting send-off to the footballer who had captured so many hearts.

Those comments about the enormity of the occasion proved correct. Streets were lined by vast crowds from the Best family home on the Cregagh Estate to Belfast's Stormont, where the service was held in the Great Hall of Parliament Buildings.

'It was one of the most touching days I have ever experienced. Hats off to the Northern Ireland parliament, they have done a fantastic job today. My love goes to the Best family; they showed fantastic dignity. You don't realise what those people have been feeling for the past week or so and they held themselves so well today. We are all proud of them. I felt very privileged. I was there to represent my club and that was well accepted by everyone,' said Sir Alex on his return.

SATURDAY 3 DECEMBER 2005

SCORERS:
Scholes 20,
Rooney 80,
Van Nistelrooy 84

ATTENDANCE:
67, 684

Barclays Premiership
Manchester United 3   Portsmouth 0

UNITED: VAN DER SAR, BROWN, FERDINAND, SILVESTRE, O'SHEA (RICHARDSON 46), PARK (SAHA 79), SMITH, SCHOLES, GIGGS (RONALDO 65), ROONEY, VAN NISTELROOY. SUBS NOT USED: HOWARD, FLETCHER.

Pity poor Pompey. Manager-less, following the departure of Alain Perrin, it was left to former Reds hero Joe Jordan to bring them to Manchester amid rumours that Harry Redknapp was on his way back to Fratton Park. They chose the wrong day to come.

If United had been finding it hard to score at home in recent matches, they had no problems this time, chalking up their biggest league win since the season began, and for Paul Scholes it was the time to end a personal goal famine that stretched back to May Day of the previous campaign.

Before kick-off, following the pattern set at West Ham six days earlier, a packed house of 67,684 stood and applauded to celebrate the life of George Best, something that continued throughout the game as United turned on a display the maestro would have been proud of. Ryan Giggs returned following his cheekbone injury and quickly found his touch with some strong attacking runs down the left flank.

'From a personal point of view it was great to start the game and the main thing for us was to get the right result,' he said.

With twenty minutes gone, he laid on the goal for Scholes who met a Giggs corner to head home. A goal rush looked on the cards, but while the chances came it was not until the eightieth minute that United added a second. By then Giggs had been replaced by Cristiano Ronaldo and Louis Saha had taken over from Ji-sung Park, completing three substitutions that began when Kieran Richardson was brought on at the start of the second half for John O'Shea. Saha's introduction was electrifying.

Within seconds he laid on the second goal, beating two defenders before trying to pick out van Nistelrooy. Full-back Andy Griffin intercepted, but could not prevent the ball reaching Rooney, who belted it into the bottom corner. With the pressure off, United made it 3–0 six minutes from time as van Nistelrooy scored after a high-speed move involving Ronaldo that was started by Scholes.

Back again, Giggs reflected on his first hour of football for six weeks.

'At 1–0, you know you are never really safe. We were always looking to get that second goal. Portsmouth were trying to get the equaliser, which left gaps at the back and we managed to capitalise on that, but overall we are pleased with the performance and obviously pleased with the result.'

After a fourth Premiership victory in a row, were things on the up?

'Yes, I think so. Our away form has been very good, it's probably here at Old Trafford that we haven't produced the kind of results we would have liked to. Hopefully we can go on a roll now at home. There are a lot of games coming up in December and we hope we can pull back the lead Chelsea hold at the moment.

'I was pleased Paul finally got his goal. His form over the past few weeks has been very good and we all know of Scholesy's reputation for getting in the box and scoring goals. I thought he was outstanding today. Obviously the icing on the cake is getting that goal and I am delighted for him. It wasn't a rehearsed move. I just thought I would try something different instead of just whipping the cross in. I floated the ball over, Rio moved towards the near post and took a few players with him and that left Scholesy with some space to run in and he just put it in the back of the net.'

The win took United to thirty points, two ahead of third-placed Liverpool, three in front of Tottenham. They had a game in hand on Chelsea who, after beating Middlesbrough earlier in the day, still held that ten-point advantage.

Whether that gap could be closed remained to be seen, but right now United had matters of more immediate importance to deal with. Next up was the Champions League game in Lisbon, where a win would see them through to the competition's knock-out phase – a draw might also be enough – but defeat would mean the end of the campaign.

As the players prepared to fly out, it was Ryan Giggs who again acted as spokesman.

'We are looking forward to it. It's an important game for the club and we were glad to get Saturday's game against Portsmouth out of the way so we can concentrate on it. We know we need the right performance and the right result. I feel we are in good shape at the moment; there are a lot of other players coming back: Gary, Louis. December is an important time. Obviously first and foremost is Benfica on Wednesday and we've got a good squad going over there and we're confident of getting a result. We want to go forward in Europe.

'You have seen the teams who are already in the hat and they are just quality teams and we want to be in that draw, so we know we need to win and we are capable of doing it if we play well. We are definitely capable of doing it.'

Chelsea, Arsenal and holders Liverpool were among those to

book a place in the next phase before the closing round of games. Also through were Barcelona, Juventus, Bayern Munich and Inter Milan. It was going to be quite a party and United were anxious for an invitation.

Sir Alex was in bullish mood, refusing to countenance the possibility that United might go out: 'I am not contemplating that. I don't even think that way. We'll be in the knockout stage, don't worry about that. We will be into the next round.'

Also confident was Cristiano Ronaldo and he looked forward to the trip more than the rest of the squad. It was a trip home, although he was uncertain of the welcome awaiting him, having played for Benfica's biggest rivals Sporting Lisbon before his switch to England.

'I don't know what kind of reception I will get. This is Benfica's stadium after all, but no way will I, or my team-mates, be intimidated. We are used to playing in these kinds of environments. It doesn't matter where we play; the atmosphere is always the same. What happens in the stadium will have no effect on our performance. The demands of the situation mean that everyone must be focused on the game and I aim to help the team win.

'We have some of our most experienced players back now. That has to be good news for the team and it means we will be a lot stronger tomorrow than we have been before.'

The game was the closing episode of a story that had unfolded over the past thirteen days: the final link with the life of George Best.

West Ham and memories of that 6–1 win, West Brom and his debut game, Portsmouth, where he was a regular visitor and a close friend of chairman Milan Mandaric, and now Benfica, who figured in his two greatest triumphs. Even in death, George's timing was sheer perfection.

United were flying out in circumstances similar to those which faced the team in 1966 when the club made its last competitive visit to Lisbon on the night George Best became a footballing legend.

Then they took with them a slender 3–2 first leg lead, in the days when every European Cup tie was sudden death. The odds were stacked against the English side, but United returned in triumph, 5–1 winners, thanks largely to a young man named Best, whose performance mesmerised a Portuguese media who, because of his fashionable flowing locks, dubbed him 'El Beatle'.

Tomorrow, United needed another chart-topping performance.

WEDNESDAY 7 DECEMBER 2005

SCORER:
Scholes 6
ATTENDANCE:
61,000

UEFA Champions League, Group Stage
Benfica 2   Manchester United 1

UNITED: VAN DER SAR, NEVILLE, FERDINAND, SILVESTRE, O'SHEA (RICHARDSON 85), RONALDO (PARK 67), SCHOLES, SMITH, GIGGS (SAHA 61), ROONEY, VAN NISTELROOY. SUBS NOT USED: HOWARD, BROWN, FLETCHER, BARDSLEY.

There was enough optimism in the camp to carry United through and things went to plan when Paul Scholes opened the scoring after six minutes.

It was the perfect send-off in Benfica's new Estadio Da Luz – the original Stadium of Light (Sunderland fans please note!) – which continues a dynasty, having been built on a site overlapping the club's former headquarters.

United had triumphed there. Was history about to repeat itself?

Statistics showed that the nineteen-year-old Best had also scored after six minutes, added a second six minutes later and laid on a third for John Connelly with a quarter of an hour gone. Not tonight. As the twelfth minute passed, it remained 1–0 to United.

Scholes had got his goal after running onto a Gary Neville cross, making it the perfect start for the full-back in his role as the club's new captain, having been officially handed the responsibility five days earlier. It was Neville's first Champions League outing of the campaign and his inclusion marked one of two changes made by the manager, with Wes Brown stepping down to make way for him and Cristiano Ronaldo taking over from Ji-sung Park.

Benfica were stunned by the early goal and reacted. In deafening noise they poured forward, forcing United onto the back foot and, in the seventeenth minute, their efforts paid dividends with an equaliser of the highest quality. It was created by Nelson, their right-back, who broke down the right, and was finished by Geovani. The Brazilian read the cross perfectly, throwing himself full length and sending a screaming header past van der Sar.

From then on United were pushed back by a series of enthusiastic raids and, in the thirty-fourth minute, the fatal blow was struck. Scholes and Wayne Rooney went close, then play switched to the other end, and Benfica took the lead through another of their Brazilians; this time Beto, who hit a speculative volley when a clearance from Alan Smith dropped near him. The ball flew goalwards, taking a wicked deflection off Scholes and giving van der Sar no chance.

United's efforts to get back came to nothing. Park was brought on after sixty-seven minutes to replace Ronaldo, whose every move had brought screams of derision from the Benfica hordes. Targeted throughout by abuse he clearly understood, he responded with a one-fingered gesture aimed towards those fans screaming at him from behind the dug out; the action was missed by officials, but not by television cameras.

United were out of Europe. Well and truly.

Villarreal won the group with Benfica second, but because Lille had beaten United in Paris, although the two sides were level on points, the French side pushed the Reds into bottom place. There was not even the consolation of entry into the UEFA Cup, which went with third place.

'We are hurting. Of course we are hurting, but we haven't performed well throughout the six games, not just this one. We are paying the consequences,' said a disconsolate Edwin van der Sar. His words were echoed by captain Neville: 'Qualifying for the knockout stages of the Champions League has been par for the course for us, but we just haven't been good enough in this group. We know what to expect over the next few days; people are going to criticise us, and rightly so, because our performances haven't been up to standard, but we have to stick together.'

The flight home was understandably subdued and later Ryan Giggs reflected on what might have been.

'We have been used to European nights at Old Trafford, going out there and dominating teams and scoring lots of goals, but we just didn't score enough. It was as simple as that. We scored three goals. That just isn't good enough, but even with that we nearly qualified. Had we scored more goals we would have got through.

'It is very hard to take. Nobody expected it, but you have got to give credit to the other teams. Villarreal did well. They were a strong team, whereas before the group phase began everybody thought they would struggle. You always get surprises in every Champions League season. Porto were the surprise package a couple of years ago, probably Liverpool in some respect last year were a surprise, going on and winning it. There have been surprises because the competition is getting stronger.

'You have got the established teams – Milan, Barcelona, Juventus, Real Madrid, ourselves – but other teams are coming through now with confidence. It is getting harder every year.'

The knives were out. As Gary Neville predicted, the rest of the week saw headlines suggesting Sir Alex's future was in doubt, fingers pointed at various players and claims that it was the end of an era at Old Trafford. As the players went through their final preparations for the first return fixture of the season, and the visit of Everton, Carlos Queiroz responded, taking a different view of things.

'Life is about lessons, you learn every day, but we were ready for that because as professionals with a long time in the game, we know what is going on, how to rebound, how to turn this into a positive thing. We are sure the team will be ready on Sunday to show that it was an accident on Wednesday.

'We have said we are disappointed, because if the fans are not happy we are not happy because we don't reach the second stage of this competition. We share that feeling. There is a sad atmosphere, of course. We are sad for that criticism, that responsibility, but our job is to guarantee and make sure we are ready to rebound and ready to perform well on Sunday.

'That is why we are professionals, because you can't be in this game only to enjoy the beautiful part of positive results and trophies. When you are a professional, when you are a champion, you must be ready to rebound in this moment and guarantee that tomorrow will be a different day. It is a time for delivery, not a time for excuses or explanations.

'We are still only in December. We played six Champions League games at a very difficult moment for us. We had an average of seven players missing, eight, sometimes nine important players injured. Think about that. Think about another team in Europe, Milan or Barcelona, and take ten major players out of their team and think of what we have been doing without making excuses for ourselves, without explanations, just moving forward, because we believe in our players, trust our players and trust our preparation.

'We are not in the Champions League, but we are second in the league and we can control that position. We can control the FA Cup and we can control the Carling Cup because it is in our hands to win that trophy, too. We can judge our season when it finishes in May, not now, and we believe that at the end of the season it will have been a great season for us.'

Three days after Everton, United were due to face Wigan Athletic at Old Trafford, the game in hand they had on Chelsea. Win both and the gap at the top would be down to seven points.

Sir Alex's deputy took a philosophical view of the situation.

'We can control the three points away against Chelsea, we can control the three points for the game we have missed and we can control our next game against Everton. Our arithmetic is a little bit more tight for Chelsea, because we know we have six points in our hands plus the three points of Sunday. We believe our job is not to put Chelsea under pressure, but to put Manchester United in the right direction. We don't want to lose time thinking about putting pressure on A, B, C ... this is not our job.

'We want to put pressure on ourselves and we can do that by winning the next three points. That would put three points in our left hand with six more there to take with our right. Take three with the left, pick up six with the right and move forward. This is all we should do.'

SUNDAY 11 DECEMBER 2005

SCORER:
Giggs 15
ATTENDANCE:
67, 831

Barclays Premiership
Manchester United 1   Everton 1

UNITED: VAN DER SAR, NEVILLE, FERDINAND, SILVESTRE, RICHARDSON (ROSSI 79), PARK (RONALDO 64), SMITH (FLETCHER 74), SCHOLES, GIGGS, ROONEY, SAHA. SUBS NOT USED: HOWARD, BROWN.

Sir Alex's hopes of a 100 per cent run through the Christmas games came crashing down at the first hurdle. The Benfica hangover appeared to have had an effect on everyone. Before kick-off, the home fans were in a subdued mood, rising occasionally to the baiting of Everton's boisterous support, and with Ruud van Nistelrooy serving a one-match suspension, the strike force struggled to score the extra goal needed to see them through.

Poor marking allowed James McFadden to put Everton in front after only seven minutes and while United huffed and puffed, the best they could muster was a Ryan Giggs equaliser with a quarter of an hour gone which, disappointingly, was followed by seventy-five minutes of missed opportunities and frustration.

Phil Neville was given the expected warm welcome on his first return to Old Trafford as an Evertonian, while Wayne Rooney got the usual berating from those who once worshipped him. United had countless chances, with Paul Scholes – who laid on the equaliser – Alan Smith, Neville, Rooney and Saha all going close, but the crucial second goal would not come.

Goalscorer Giggs was stunned by the stalemate: 'With the chances we created throughout the game, I can't believe we didn't win, but in saying that, when your chances come you have to put them away, especially when you are playing at home. That isn't the first time that's happened at Old Trafford this season, but away from home we have had no problem scoring.

'The lads are disappointed because we played well, worked hard, but just couldn't put the ball in the back of the net. I don't know what it is. They are good chances we are creating, so we have just got to carry on and hopefully goals will come our way at home. One positive is that we are creating a lot of scoring opportunities and good ones at that. I am sure we will start scoring goals.'

Chelsea's lead was now twelve points and Ryan admitted it was getting close to win or bust.

'We have been saying all along that we have just got to look out for ourselves and keep winning, but we haven't managed to do that today. We have to pick ourselves up now because on Wednesday we have an important game, and over the Christmas period, with so many games, a lot of points are going to change hands. We have just got to concentrate on ourselves. I know this result is a boost for Chelsea, but our form's been good in the last six or seven games, really good. If we keep playing like we are, the goals will come.

'After the week we have had, perhaps it's a good thing we have another home game coming up as quickly as Wednesday,' Giggs added. 'But Wigan are a good team and they played well again at Chelsea yesterday [Chelsea had won 1–0, somewhat fortunately]. They work hard, so we will need to be at our best, and if chances come our way we will have to put them away.

'We have to blank out what happened today. We have another game, so it is no good thinking back and wondering what could have been, if this had happened or that. We have to look forward now to the Wigan game, because they are a hard team to beat and we will have to play well.'

There was little time to think about what might have been had United repeated their opening-day performance against Everton. Another home draw, their third of the season, meant that the Reds had picked up only twelve points from a possible twenty-one in seven games.

It had been another difficult week, but it had begun with a

glimmer of hope for one player. The night before the squad flew out to Portugal, Ole Gunnar Solskjaer made his comeback. After over two years on the sidelines, the popular Norwegian played forty-five minutes for the reserves, a giant stride for a player whose career had seemed threatened by a knee injury.

'It was good to get the first game out of the way and now I can just concentrate on the training and forget all the stories about me not playing again. I saw one in the paper two weeks ago saying I was finished and that the club was going to give me a testimonial, but nothing shocks you any more in football. I know my own situation and I knew it was only press stories.

'Now I have just got to fine tune. All the hard work's been done, like the plodding on the treadmill in the gym and everything now, it's the sharpening and the fine-tuning of the form. It's back to football training and being out there with the lads is such a big step up for me. I am just going to enjoy every single minute being out there training, enjoying the wind and the rain, everything.'

Had there been any dark moments?

'It depends on how you define dark. It has been a long plod, but I have been really good, I think.'

What next?

'Right now I am planning to go into the physio's room and wipe my name off the injured list, because Rob [the physio] just said to me that I'm discharged. That's the main thing, then let's see from there.'

As Solskjaer continued his build-up and the rest of his teammates prepared for the next game, Sir Alex decided it was time the club hit back at some of the adverse publicity it had been receiving. He cut his press conference with the national press drastically short saying little more than: 'Wigan have done well and I'm looking forward to the challenge.' He then explained his actions to local radio.

He had had enough of the sniping.

'I know exactly where this is coming from. Within sections of the media there is a hatred of Manchester United that has always been there. I can understand it a little because we are such a high-profile club and it comes with the territory I suppose. But they go over the top. They try to fragment the club; the players from the supporters and the supporters from the players. Our fans are aware of that and they will not fall into that trap.

'I make the point strongly – when we are at our best is when the fans are right behind us. That is the only thing that should matter. Sticking together is the key for us.'

The manager felt he had good reason to hit back. According to most back pages, United were having a terrible season, yet they had accumulated more points at this stage of the season than they had in four of the previous six campaigns and two more points after fifteen games than they had on the way to the Treble of 1998–99. The difference? Chelsea.

'We all have a problem because Chelsea's consistent form makes it difficult for us to win the league. In any normal season, most of the teams below Chelsea would think they are doing quite well, but we must continue to play football and enjoy the game. If we do that, eventually things will come right.'

Wayne Rooney also remained confident.

'Sunday was disappointing, but Chelsea can be caught. We are hoping we can win all our games from now on and that they slip up and we can capitalise on it. The confidence is still there. We all believe in ourselves and we have a squad that's good enough. Perhaps one good result will spark everything off and this could be it.

'I've seen Wigan a couple of times and they've done well. Paul Jewell's done a fantastic job and deserves all the praise he is getting. They're a strong team and work hard together and all credit to them and hopefully that can continue – after our game! We know it'll be tough, but we've got to turn them over.'

Wigan had proved the surprise package of the Premiership since winning promotion in May. They had come within sixty seconds of the major shock of holding Chelsea to a draw in their first game at the highest level and sat sixth in the table, above clubs like Arsenal, Newcastle, Manchester City and Everton.

With so much local interest, it was little wonder the first Greater

Manchester derby between the two clubs attracted 67,793 to Old Trafford.

WEDNESDAY 14 DECEMBER 2005

SCORERS:
Ferdinand 30,
Rooney 35, 55,
Van Nistelrooy 70
(pen)

ATTENDANCE:
67,793

Barclays Premiership
Manchester United 4   Wigan Athletic 0

UNITED: VAN DER SAR, NEVILLE, FERDINAND (BARDSLEY 65), BROWN, O'SHEA, FLETCHER, SMITH, SCHOLES (PARK 74), GIGGS (RONALDO 70), ROONEY, VAN NISTELROOY. SUBS NOT USED: HOWARD, SAHA.

Crisis, what crisis? Jeers turned to cheers as United made light of all that talk about Sir Alex's future and the Old Trafford goal drought ended in style. Another standing ovation for the manager before kick-off was followed by a repeat for the players as they left the pitch at the end. In between times, there had been a vibrant display of attacking football by both teams.

Wigan made a fight of it even though they had been totally out-punched by the rampant Reds, who had several chances before going ahead. It took half an hour for a goal to come, but it was worth waiting for as far as Rio Ferdinand was concerned, with the England defender getting his first for United on his 140th appearance, heading home a Giggs corner. Five minutes later, Mike Pollitt, the Wigan 'keeper who began his career as a United trainee, was picking the ball out of his net again, this time after some great work by Rooney, whose shot was unstoppable.

In the second half, Rooney hit the bar from four yards out, van Nistelrooy missed a chance as Pollitt saved, but the two combined after fifty-five minutes, with Wayne chipping the 'keeper after a lay-off from the Dutchman. It was van Nistelrooy who rounded things off with a seventieth-minute penalty. The three points won saw United stepping over Liverpool and back into second place, nine points behind Chelsea.

'I wouldn't say that was the best we have played this season, we have had some good performances, but the difference was we got that second goal and that settled us down,' said a satisfied Sir Alex. 'It gave us the confidence and brought back the swagger of our game and some of the football after that was terrific. Missing chances at home put us in a dangerous situation on Sunday against Everton, when Wayne Rooney could have scored five. Tonight he might have scored four but got two and that settled us down and won the match for us.

'I just hope we can go on a consistent run now. We've had a bad week and we hope we are out of it. It isn't an easy league and we will go on and get through December. When we get to Arsenal on 3 January, we will have a better picture of where we lie.'

The following day Roy Keane was in the news again as his move to Celtic was completed. The former Old Trafford favourite signed an eighteen-month deal to play in Scotland, topping off the move with words some United fans would not have enjoyed reading.

'It's a great move for me. I feel that this is where I belong and I'm here to work hard and win games. I've been in the Premiership for a long time and feel I have proved myself there and needed a different environment, different teams, different grounds. Every boy in Ireland has an interest in Celtic, although my English team at the time was Spurs for some reason!'

For Keane's old club there was a busy schedule ahead. Next up was the trip to Aston Villa, three days later Birmingham City in the quarter-finals of the Carling Cup, then the Christmas games of West Bromwich Albion at Old Trafford on Boxing Day, a second visit to Birmingham, this time for the Premiership fixture, and on 31 December, Bolton Wanderers at Old Trafford. Win them all and who knows what 2006 might have in store?

Sir Alex outlined the task ahead: 'December is always an important month. If you get to the end of it in a challenging position you know you have a real chance. It's a crucial month. We have nine games. Most clubs are the same, although we had the Wigan match, which was rescheduled. It's never been any different.

'You are not getting any respite whatsoever. You have to deal with the situation of when you make the changes and where you make them. Defenders can survive and get through it, midfield players have a task, and front players, in terms of keeping the freshness for them, is another issue. I have always said that by the time you get to the end of this month you have an idea where you stand.'

At Villa Park, United stood tall.

SATURDAY 17 DECEMBER 2005

SCORERS:
Van Nistelrooy 10,
Rooney 51

ATTENDANCE:
37,128

Barclays Premiership
Aston Villa 0   Manchester United 2

UNITED: VAN DER SAR, NEVILLE, FERDINAND, BROWN, O'SHEA, PARK, FLETCHER, SCHOLES, GIGGS (RONALDO 63), ROONEY, VAN NISTELROOY. SUBS NOT USED: HOWARD, BARDSLEY, ROSSI, R. JONES.

Two down three to go. The Reds stayed on course for that 100 per cent Premiership performance over Christmas as they slashed Chelsea's lead to six points – but perhaps not for long. This game kicked off at 12.45 p.m., with Chelsea facing Arsenal the following day, but hopes were high something might happen in the London derby after Ruud van Nistelrooy put United in front in the tenth minute and Wayne Rooney added the second six minutes into the second half for a comfortable win.

Sir Alex made one change to the side that had put four past Wigan, with Ji-sung Park taking over from Alan Smith in midfield, while Ritchie Jones, who had scored in United's 5–0 reserve league win over Bolton Wanderers in midweek, earned a seat on the bench. Darren Fletcher made the opener with a defence-splitting pass to Ruud van Nistelrooy, who brushed his marker aside before firing home. Then Park prised Villa open with a perfect pass to Rooney who shot low and accurately to tie up the points.

Sunday morning was spent making plans for Tuesday's game at St Andrews, as the Carling Cup pitted Sir Alex against another of his former charges. After Bryan Robson in the last round, there was

Steve Bruce in this and the Reds boss planned to resort to his normal approach to the competition.

'We'll be making a few changes to the side that played in the last round and the one that played at Villa. I'll play all the young players, Rossi, Pique, Bardsley, and by that I am also talking about Darren Fletcher, John O'Shea and Cristiano Ronaldo. The younger ones can handle it, no problem. These players have got plenty of the attributes needed for this type of game. They are young, they are fresh and they are fit, so that will be the same as last time really.

'I don't know how Stevie is going to approach the match because there is always that incentive for Birmingham, who haven't won a trophy for years, but I will be using the young players. Even so, the team I play will definitely be out to win it.'

Following the early exit from Europe and Chelsea's lead in the Premiership, did the domestic cups take on greater importance?

'I have never given that a thought. The important thing at our club is always to try to do well in all the tournaments. The Carling Cup has always been viewed differently, of course, but what we did last season applies this year.'

In the previous campaign, Sir Alex had rotated his squad. The 'fringe' players faced Crewe and Crystal Palace in the first two games, with a stronger side beating Arsenal in the quarter-final, before the Reds bowed out to Chelsea in the semis, losing at Old Trafford after a 0–0 draw at Stamford Bridge.

TUESDAY 20 DECEMBER 2005

Carling Cup, Fifth Round
Birmingham City 1   Manchester United 3

SCORERS:
Saha 46, 63,
Park 50

UNITED: HOWARD, NEVILLE, BROWN, SILVESTRE (FERDINAND 66), RICHARDSON, RONALDO, FLETCHER, O'SHEA (R. JONES 66), PARK, ROSSI (ROONEY 46), SAHA. SUBS NOT USED: VAN DER SAR, BARDSLEY.

ATTENDANCE:
20,454

Two goals from Louis Saha booked a place in the semi-finals in a game the Reds never looked like losing, despite the blank first half.

Sir Alex made his predicted changes, with Tim Howard, Louis Saha, Kieran Richardson, Mikael Silvestre, Cristiano Ronaldo and Giuseppe Rossi all drafted in. There was also a familiar face among the opposition, as Nicky Butt lined up against his old club.

With United looking for a goal, Wayne Rooney replaced Giuseppe Rossi after the break and his presence swiftly paid dividends, but it was not the Merseysider who scored. Ji-sung Park began the move, finding Ronaldo on the right and his low cross was stabbed home by Saha to lift some of the tension. Four minutes later it was 2–0, with Saha again involved, this time Park finishing the move after an inter-changing of passes between the two.

United's ticket for the semi-final came in the sixty-third minute with a tremendous goal from Saha, who ran onto the perfectly deliv-ered final ball from Gary Neville to send it flying into the net. Birmingham pulled one back through Jiri Jarosik with fifteen min-utes remaining, but it was too little too late from the home side.

When the draw for the semi-final paired Arsenal with Wigan Athletic and United with Blackburn Rovers, some experts predicted a Carling Cup final repeat of May's FA Cup showdown at the Millennium Stadium, when United lost to the Gunners in a penalty shoot-out. Others saw Blackburn as a major threat to the Reds. Had they not already beaten them at Old Trafford? Whatever the out-come, it meant that, for a third successive round, a club managed by a former United player stood between Sir Alex and another final. Bryan Robson, Steve Bruce, and now Mark Hughes.

'They are all doing their job well,' said the mentor of Manchester. 'It's a hard job and I like to see them do well.'

Ruud van Nistelrooy saw Blackburn as presenting a stiff chal-lenge. 'It's always a special game against Blackburn. I remember the last time we reached the League Cup final we played them in the semis as well. They were hard games. We drew at home and won away, but we know what we are facing.'

Before that was the Christmas rush, and the usual glut of games jammed in over the holiday period. That was something the Dutch striker had to adjust to after moving to England.

'With four games coming up in eight days, it's important to prepare for them. In Holland there aren't any games at this time of year,
but I suppose I have got used to it now. This is my fifth season here
and I don't know any different really, but we could do with a break
somewhere in the season. It will be more playing, recovery work and
not too much training. You just eat well after a game, try to get as
much food into you as you can, then rest and do some light training
until the next game.'

After he and Wayne Rooney had scored in the last two
Premiership games, van Nistelrooy was keen to get things going
again after missing the Carling tie at Birmingham. He felt the partnership was working well.

'It's there for everybody to see. We are both attack-minded players, but we do it in different ways. But the good thing is we comple-
ment each other. He likes to play off me, sometimes I can play off
him. Forging a partnership is not difficult. It's great to have one.
While I have been here I have had Scholesy and Solskjaer and now
Wayne and I have always played my best when I have had some guy
around me and we have scored loads of goals between us.

'This has been a good run and we want to continue that. At the
moment we are doing well, but it's always the next game where it
counts.'

The manager's pre-Christmas conference covered two games. The
Boxing Day visit of Albion and a second meeting with Bryan Robson
in just over three weeks, then the return to Bruce's Birmingham for
a Premiership outing two days later.

'Those Carling Cup games have no bearing on these games. When
we played West Brom both teams made changes, so it will be a different type of game on Monday, whereas Steve had so many injuries
he didn't have his strongest team out on Tuesday.'

The weekend came and went and as most of the country gorged
itself on turkey, it was training as usual for the players on Christmas
Day.

MONDAY 26 DECEMBER 2005

SCORERS:
Scholes 35,
Ferdinand 45,
Van Nistelrooy 63

ATTENDANCE:
67,972

Barclays Premiership
Manchester United 3   West Bromwich Albion 0

UNITED: VAN DER SAR, NEVILLE, FERDINAND, BROWN (RICHARDSON 46), O'SHEA, PARK, FLETCHER, SCHOLES (SMITH 61), GIGGS, ROONEY, VAN NISTELROOY (SAHA 66). SUBS NOT USED: HOWARD, BARDSLEY.

With Chelsea beating Fulham before this game kicked off, the pressure was on to make certain the unbeaten run stretched to nine games ... it did. Paul Scholes got the first goal and Ruud van Nistelrooy the third, while in between Rio Ferdinand made it two in two home games after finally finding his scoring touch.

It was just not Albion's day. They lost defender Paul Robinson through injury in the first half, after a bone-crunching collision with team-mate Thomas Gaardsoe, and it was anything but a joyful return to Old Trafford for old boys Jonathan Greening and Ronnie Wallwork as Albion battled to stay in the game.

Both teams made six changes to the sides fielded in the Carling Cup, but little changed as far as the outcome was concerned, with United again running the show.

Ferdinand was not only a scorer but a creator, having a hand in the first goal, running strongly upfield before leaving Ji-sung Park to continue a move that Scholes expertly finished. The second came during stoppage time for the injury to Robinson, when Ryan Giggs took a corner on the right and an unmarked Rio headed home. An hour gone and Alan Smith came into the action and, within a minute, laid on the third with a cross from the right, which van Nistelrooy's head met perfectly.

The January transfer window was four days away when United made the return trip to Birmingham, but in typical Ferguson style, Sir Alex was keeping his cards close to his chest. There were hints he might take an uncustomary plunge for new players to swell the squad after the early season struggle to fill injury gaps, but there was nothing definite.

'I don't know if we will or not, I'm just looking at the situation at the moment,' was now his approach, a month after declaring: 'We are actually playing the numbers game. It is lack of numbers and this is possibly where we will be looking at the January window. We are down on numbers more than anything.'

One player linked to Old Trafford was Nemanja Vidic, the Spartak Moscow defender, another was Deportivo La Coruna's Argentinean ace Aldo Duscher. With both their clubs out of Europe, there was speculation that they might be willing to do business.

WEDNESDAY 28 DECEMBER 2005

Barclays Premiership
Birmingham City 2   Manchester United 2

UNITED: VAN DER SAR, NEVILLE, FERDINAND, O'SHEA, RICHARDSON (GIGGS 86), FLETCHER, SMITH (PARK 84), SCHOLES, RONALDO (SOLSKJAER 84), ROONEY, VAN NISTELROOY. SUBS NOT USED: HOWARD, PIQUE.

SCORERS:
Van Nistelrooy 4,
Rooney 53

ATTENDANCE:
28,459

All good things must end, but this was a major blow to any aspirations of catching Chelsea, even though Ruud and Rooney were once again on thrilling form. United led twice, but Birmingham would not lie down, and the game could have gone either way after the home side levelled with thirteen minutes to play.

Van Nistelrooy gave United the lead after only four minutes, with Kieran Richardson breaking down the left before crossing low for Ruud to slide home under pressure from Matthew Upson. The first equaliser came when Nicky Butt robbed Ronaldo deep inside the Birmingham half and found Jamie Clapham, whose run ended with his first goal since joining the Blues.

Rooney was next to score, eight minutes into the second half, making light of slippery conditions as he guided home Alan Smith's cross, but Birmingham's persistence paid off and fifteen minutes from time, when Walter Pandiani replaced Jermaine Pennant, the substitution proved decisive. Pandiani levelled within three minutes after getting on the end of Neil Kilkenny's right-wing cross.

While the result provided a lifeline for Birmingham, for United it was two valuable points dropped. As news filtered through that Chelsea had beaten Manchester City 1–0 at Eastlands, Sir Alex had a clear picture of the task ahead: the season had reached its halfway stage with nineteen games played and United were in second place, but eleven points adrift of the leaders.

'It's a mountain, a real mountain, but you have to give credit to Chelsea. One-nils seem to be a great psychological challenge to them. We had the game watched and apparently it was a dull affair, but they got their goal at the end and it came from three ricochets. You get breaks like that when you are up at the top. We had them during our spell.

'Luck's an important part when you are doing well,' he added.

The manager had double reason to look forward to the next game. Firstly, came the opportunity to share an after-match drink with Sam Allardyce, the Bolton boss who is a close friend, but secondly, the two could raise a glass to celebrate Sir Alex's sixty-fourth birthday on the day the year ended.

SATURDAY 31 DECEMBER 2005

SCORERS:
Own goal 8,
Saha 44,
Ronaldo 68, 90

ATTENDANCE:
67,858

Barclays Premiership
Manchester United 4   Bolton Wanderers 1

UNITED: VAN DER SAR, NEVILLE, FERDINAND, SILVESTRE, RICHARDSON, RONALDO, FLETCHER (PIQUE 85), O'SHEA, GIGGS, ROONEY (PARK 79), SAHA (VAN NISTELROOY 79). SUBS NOT USED: HOWARD, BARDSLEY.

The Reds saw out the year in style with Louis Saha taking a giant stride towards 2006. Back to full fitness, he celebrated Hogmanay in style with his first Premiership goal since 21 January.

'It's a fact that every time I look back I see a bad experience, but with that you have to think, "that's life", and you gain experience from it. It effects you because you can't get any confidence, so it's difficult, but when you have a club like this you can always get that confidence, not just about football but about your lifestyle, so I am happy with that.

'It wasn't like being injured once or twice; I was out for a long time, so it was very easy to think I might not get the chance to show the fans what I could do, but I think I did great to let it go and have a shot at it.'

Ruud van Nistelrooy was dropped to the bench to make way for Saha and the French star made his intentions clear from the start. With eight minutes gone, Louis was breathing down Bruno N'Gotty's neck, forcing him to turn a Richardson cross into his own net for the opening goal.

Bolton came back, with Gary Speed nipping in on the far post to head home a flicked-on throw-in after thirty-three minutes, then things tilted United's way again. Ronaldo hit a post, then, when Ben Haim tried to head a long clearance from van der Sar back to Jaaskelainen, Saha nipped in and took the ball past the 'keeper to restore the lead.

In the second half, Ronaldo again hit a post with a long-range shot, but his effort was rewarded five minutes later, when Rooney set him up after a powerful run. At 3–1 United were in control and, almost on the final whistle, Ronaldo scored his second – he might have had four – with substitutes Gerard Pique and van Nistelrooy combining before picking out the Portuguese star who beat his man before scoring.

For skipper Neville the end of 2005 was a time for reflection. 'The way that everyone at the club will look at it will be that it was a year when we didn't achieve what we wanted to. We didn't win any trophies in 2005 and that always means a bad year for the club. There has been a lot of negative coverage of Manchester United, some of it generated by ourselves, some of it the sort of stuff you always expect when you don't win trophies, and the only people capable of relieving the club of that are the players.

'When you win trophies all the peripheral matters seem to get lost, but they get blown out of all proportion when you aren't winning. We don't ask to be protected from the criticism. We realise we are playing at the biggest club in the world and with that comes the biggest coverage, the biggest responsibilities, the biggest expectations and rightly so. I don't go along with the theory that we have been spoilt over the last ten years, but what has happened is what this club should be achieving. We should be winning championships, European Cups, FA Cups and that is what we have to continue to do.

'You accept that you can't win every year. You know that is going to happen because no team ever has, but over a period of time you know we have to win trophies. We have always been in contention. Last season we were very unlucky against Arsenal in the FA Cup final. We deserved to win that match, but it has been one of those years where, to be honest, we have underachieved. We have been inconsistent in the league, but to be eleven points behind and having lost only two games?

'We said last year that the bar had been raised and that is certainly the case. Chelsea have won eighteen out of twenty games and that is phenomenal. It's relentless. But it is giving people the opportunity to be negative about our performances a lot more easily than they could be in the past. We have to maintain the points tally we got in championship-winning seasons and we will either get to their level, or they will come down to ours. Going into 2006 we have to do better.'

CHAPTER SIX

A cupful of woe as a domestic Double disappears

Traditionally, New Year begins with first footing – the action of bringing good luck to a household early on 1 January, by taking the inaugural stride over its doorstep. For United, 2006 started with a last footing.

The year was three days old when they faced Arsenal at Highbury for the final league game between the two clubs at the famous London stadium. Arsenal would be moving to bigger, better surroundings in the summer, but all the talk of them playing catch-up with United held no weight as far as Sir Alex was concerned. His comments were a little tongue in cheek, but he showed the Season of Goodwill was ending by announcing that no matter how plush the Gunners' new stadium might be they would still be years behind the Reds.

'Rival United? They would need three stadiums and thirty-three teams to rival us as a club. They will never be as big as Manchester United. Never. It will give them more attendances maybe, but I don't know if they will be able to get 60,000 every week. We are a big club. We are well known all over the world. Don't forget, United's supporters branches started in places like Malta way back in 1958. The real story started in 1968 when they won the European Cup and the recovery after Munich.

'United have produced more world-class players than any other club in Britain and more players who have played for their country.

We have established ourselves without question as one of the great clubs in the world. You can measure things any way that you like, winning trophies and the rest of it, but there is no question that United will always be in people's minds as a great club.'

Was Sir Alex playing mind games? Perhaps. But with Chelsea romping away and Arsenal eleven points behind United, for the first time in years this game was going to have no significant impact on the top of table. Or was it?

'You never know. What I have said in the past few weeks is that we want to be the closest to Chelsea if they do slip up. The thing about all the teams apart from them is that no one this season has had consistency like theirs and credit to them for that. Arsenal have had bad periods, we have had bad periods, Liverpool have had bad periods, but if Chelsea do a Devon Loch [the horse that famously collapsed in the run-in at the Grand National] then we want to be the closest team to them.'

In February 2005, United had stunned Arsenal by winning 4–2 at Highbury, and Sir Alex would happily have settled for the same as his players stepped out on a chilly north London night.

TUESDAY 3 JANUARY 2006

ATTENDANCE:
38,313

Barclays Premiership
Arsenal 0   Manchester United 0

UNITED: VAN DER SAR, NEVILLE, FERDINAND, BROWN, SILVESTRE, RONALDO, FLETCHER, O'SHEA, GIGGS (PARK 73), ROONEY, VAN NISTELROOY. SUBS NOT USED: HOWARD, SAHA, BARDSLEY, PIQUE.

Not quite the start to the New Year that Sir Alex wanted, but there have been many times he would gladly have settled for a point from this game. Chance-wise, United won hands down, but neither side could complain when the spoils were shared come the final whistle. Without Roy Keane and Patrick Vieira, both now in pastures new, the game lacked its usual fire and whether that will be rekindled when life starts for the Gunners in Ashburton Grove remains to be seen.

Wayne Rooney and Cristiano Ronaldo were lively and Arsenal went close when Thierry Henry's free-kick flew wide of Edwin van der Sar's dive as well as the post, bringing United physio Rob Swire into the action with the 'keeper taking a knock as he fell.

United should have gone ahead in the forty-fourth minute, when a Ruud van Nistelrooy beauty came off Jens Lehmann and ran to Ronaldo, who could not keep his shot down. Rooney sent a looping header over the top, Ronaldo's crosses caused chaos all evening and Ryan Giggs, van Nistelrooy and full-back Neville all had scoring chances. The game ended with United pressing and Wes Brown's powerful header cleared off the line by Emmanuel Eboue.

Sir Alex did his best to confuse the issue, but in the end made an early move to strengthen his squad as the month-long transfer window opened. Nemanja Vidic was indeed a target, with the manager confirming that he would be a United player before the next game.

'The deal's been done, but it will be Thursday before the work permit comes through,' he said.

There was also talk of him landing Patrice Evra, a left-back from Monaco, with negotiations continuing as the FA Cup tie against Nationwide Conference side Burton Albion approached. As neither player was likely to be available for that game, Sir Alex turned his attention to those who were.

'Ole Gunnar Solskjaer will play, but Paul Scholes is out, he's still suffering from that blurred vision. All the rest are fit, but I will be making changes. Players like Louis Saha will feature. Cristiano, Brown, Silvestre, Tim Howard in goal. I'll be playing a strong side and it's not a matter of not taking risks, but of using your squad. Four games in eight days does take its toll.

'You can't take things for granted in the cup, but it always has its romance and for Manchester United it has had more of that than any other club in the country. We have won it more times than anyone, so it has always been a special cup to this club.'

Many romantics probably wanted non-league Burton to pull off a giant-killing act after opting to play the game at their own ground, but for once United would not be stepping into unknown territory against the minnows.

'We were down there six weeks ago to play them for the official opening of their stadium,' the manager revealed. 'One or two of the players who played that night will be in the side on Sunday, like Phil Bardsley, Gerard Pique, Giuseppe Rossi. It's a big pitch, but we have heard they are having a few problems with it.'

SUNDAY 8 JANUARY 2006

ATTENDANCE:
6,191

FA Cup, Third Round
Burton Albion 0   Manchester United 0

UNITED: HOWARD, BARDSLEY, PIQUE, BROWN, SILVESTRE, SOLSKJAER (RONALDO 59), R. JONES, O'SHEA, RICHARDSON, ROSSI (ROONEY 59), SAHA. SUBS NOT USED: STEELE, ECKERSLEY, CAMPBELL.

Those pitch problems were solved with tons of sand, but beach football or not, there was no giant-killing act, although no one could deny Nigel Clough's side had earned their club a big pay day at Old Trafford. They held out against a United side which, at the end, included both Wayne Rooney and Cristiano Ronaldo, and it was thanks only to a last-second save by Saul Deely in the Burton goal, that Ritchie Jones did not find his place in the Reds' record books.

Young Jones played the whole ninety minutes before leaving for a spell with feeder club Royal Antwerp and with Ole Gunnar Solskjaer skippering the side on his 200th competitive start, United appeared to have enough talent to have seen off the Brewers. Solskjaer's comeback continued as he played up to the fifty-eighth minute before handing the armband to an immensely proud Rooney as he came from the bench, but neither of the United captains managed to steer their side to victory.

There was drama before the kick-off when Ji-sung Park was injured during the warm-up and John O'Shea was drafted in after originally being named as a substitute; his place on the bench was

Late substitute Ole Gunnar Solskjaer was a welcome sight on the pitch against Birmingham, having been out of the side after a long absence for injury. But even he couldn't conjure a late winner in United's league fixture.

Louis Saha scores his first Premiership goal since January against Bolton on New Year's Eve to help Sir Alex have a very happy sixty-fourth birthday.

The versatile John O'Shea takes on Thierry Henry during the somewhat low-key 0–0 draw against Arsenal in United's last game at Highbury.

Gerard Pique, one of United's young stars in the making, gave a solid performance in the heart of the Reds' defence against Burton in the third round of the FA Cup.

Louis Saha strikes the opener in United's Carling Cup semi-final clash at Blackburn Rovers, as a full-strength side claimed a draw to set up the second leg at Old Trafford.

Ruud van Nistelrooy celebrates scoring only the second Carling Cup goal of his United career to give United the advantage in the second leg of their tie with Blackburn.

Cristiano Ronaldo smiles for the camera.

Patrice Evra, newly signed from Monaco, had a tough debut in the Manchester derby in January, when City emerged as 3–1 winners and United slipped sixteen points behind Chelsea, with Liverpool in hot pursuit of the runners-up place.

Ninety minutes on the clock, the ball is in the back of the net and Rio Ferdinand has scored the goal to win the match against Liverpool – cue the celebrations!

Wes Brown, Kieran Richardson and Gerard Pique celebrate with Giuseppe Rossi, after he scores the second goal in United's 5–0 victory over Burton in the third round replay.

A potentially tricky away tie at Wolves in the fourth round of the FA Cup became a little bit easier when an early Kieran Richardson goal set United on their way to a comfortable 3–0 victory.

After seventeen games in two months, Sir Alex Ferguson and Carlos Queiroz were pleased with what they saw against Fulham at the start of February.

Among the players on view was Serbian defender Nemanja Vidic, signed from Spartak Moscow, who made his home debut in the 4–2 victory over Fulham.

Cristiano Ronaldo celebrates with Ryan Giggs and Mikael Silvestre after scoring his first goal in a 3–1 triumph over Portsmouth. That goal was voted the best of the season by the fans.

Wes Brown and Gary Neville console Alan Smith as he receives treatment for a horrendous injury during United's fifth round FA Cup tie against Liverpool.

taken by reserve striker Fraizer Campbell. United never really looked like losing, while Burton managed to hold out against a second-half onslaught that would have seen many a side crumble and, for the second successive season – after Exeter City in 2005 – non-league opponents won the right to a replay.

'I loved it. Obviously the result wasn't what we hoped for, but being out there was great,' said satisfied skipper Solskjaer. 'We love the FA Cup. I have watched it on TV all my life and you know there are always going to be a few shocks, but although we were prepared for the game it just didn't happen for us.

'We knew Burton were going to give us a hard game and there was certainly no underestimation from us. We tried. You might think Premiership fitness would help, but they stuck to their guns and there will be loads of people happy for football in general, because they know results like these can happen.

'I have been looking forward to this game for a while. It was my cup final and it was great just preparing for it and knowing I was back playing again. It's what's always been in my mind when I was injured and I just wanted to get back.'

With the signings of both Vidic and Evra confirmed on the eve of the tie, Solskjaer added: 'It's good to see new players coming in. That sort of thing gives everybody a boost and a little bit of a warning sign that, if you want to be in this side, you have to perform.'

Sir Alex faced another hectic week with two more important away fixtures coming up within six days. First was the opener of the two-legged Carling Cup semi-final against Blackburn then, three days later, the Manchester derby at Eastlands. He would not be rushing in the new players.

'Vidic is only doing endurance work at present because he hasn't played since 22 November, when they went into their winter in Russia. He's working with our fitness coach, so it depends how he comes through in the next week or so. Once we can include him in the football part of training we'll know. He won't be involved on Wednesday.

'As for Evra, he gives us a different option in the left-back position. He's a good footballer. With Gaby Heinze out and Quinton Fortune's injury still a problem, it was important to bring in a left-sided player. He'll be ready almost immediately because he's only had a two-week break and he's been training through it in Monaco.'

United were two games away from a final, but Sir Alex appeared to be concentrating more on the weekend's Premiership game on the other side of Manchester, rather than on the first leg of the semi-final at Ewood Park.

'We started off against Barnet with a very young team, then we got West Brom and, because of the occasion, decided to bring in more experienced players. Against Birmingham, we played a side we hoped would get us through and that is what I will do on Wednesday.

'We will play one that sets us up for the second leg. We have enough numbers to make sure we make the right changes. At Birmingham, we included some of the first-team squad to make sure we got through and we can do the same again. Being a two-legged tie we can adapt to playing away from home, then in the return leg we can see what position we are in.'

Blackburn could not wait for the game. They had hit a winning streak since beating Middlesbrough in the quarter-finals, with three Premiership victories over Christmas followed by a 3–0 FA Cup romp against QPR. They also felt that their win at Old Trafford in September had given them the edge.

'It will be a hard game. They are in good form and it's going to be a tough semi-final. They are going to be playing their strongest side, where we won't be. We will certainly be making changes from Sunday to Wednesday and Wednesday to Saturday, because we have City in that 12.45 p.m. kick-off, but that is the beauty of having a squad.'

WEDNESDAY 11 JANUARY 2006

Carling Cup, Semi-Final First Leg
Blackburn Rovers 1   Manchester United 1

SCORER:
Saha 30

ATTENDANCE:
24,348

UNITED: VAN DER SAR, NEVILLE, FERDINAND, BROWN, SILVESTRE, RONALDO, FLETCHER (O'SHEA 85), SMITH, GIGGS, ROONEY, SAHA (VAN NISTELROOY 82). SUBS NOT USED: HOWARD, BARDSLEY, ROSSI.

Once again Louis Saha showed he was the man of the moment as far as this competition is concerned with his fourth goal in three rounds, as United took an important step towards the final. As expected, Rovers' boss Mark Hughes sent out his strongest side, making five changes to his FA Cup line-up, although one player who kept his place was Robbie Savage, who was a member of Old Trafford's 1992 'dream team', which launched David Beckham, Paul Scholes, Gary Neville and co. on the big stage.

Had Sir Alex been bluffing with all that talk of playing a weakened side?

With the exception of Ruud van Nistelrooy all the big guns were there and the Dutchman was on the bench. After a shaky start, United took the lead on the half hour thanks to a clinical finish from Saha. He ran onto a Ryan Giggs throughball to hit a low, unstoppable shot past Brad Friedel. Six minutes later, however, it was all square again.

Rovers struck back through Morten Gamst Pedersen, whose thunderous shot gave van der Sar no chance as he added to the two goals he had netted when the sides had met four months earlier to complete a unique hat-trick. A high-tension game saw eight players booked, four from each side, but try as they might, no one could come up with the winner, so everything hung on the second leg.

'We didn't start very well, so obviously it was nice to score when I did,' was Louis Saha's initial reaction as he looked back on the game. 'We were lucky not to be punished in the first five minutes, so it was good to get some nice movement going, which led to our goal. It was a shame it ended in a draw because, in the second half, we played a bit better and it's not often we go ahead and let the opposition back in. Most of the time when we get a goal, it gives us confidence and we keep going, but that wasn't the case tonight.

'It's good to get another start and another goal, but I need to keep going. Every time I get a game I try to give my maximum and it's working right now. The main thing is every time I go on the pitch I feel better. This is the first time I have had two games in a row, so obviously I tried to respond to that. This is a great opportunity to get to a final, so we expect a good game at Old Trafford and it's one we want to win.

'We would probably have taken 1–1 before the game. It's a cup-tie; Blackburn put a very strong team out and it was difficult. It's important that we try and win this trophy. We are out of the Champions League, so now every competition is important for us.'

Sir Alex explained that his change of plan had not been a bluff.

'I gave it good consideration and what I felt was, in modern day terms, Manchester United teams normally play Saturday-Wednesday-Saturday and that is the kind of player you want. Because after the Arsenal game I had not played many of them against Burton, I felt nine days was just too long. They are all happier playing and they all wanted to play, particularly in a semi-final.

'The big decision was whether I should include Ruud, but I explained to him that this is the one position when I would want to keep him for Saturday. Louis is a terrific option because a goal threat like that is always a handy thing to have.'

Wayne Rooney was one of the bookings, but dismissed an altercation with Robbie Savage, who was also shown yellow, as: 'Nothing more than handbags at ten paces. We wanted to give a performance, to get a result to take back to Old Trafford. We battled hard; it was a tough game. We should have held on, unfortunately we didn't, but we still got a good result. Because Blackburn scored not long after us that knocked us a bit, but we have done well defensively, we were solid. I could have done a lot better, some of it was good, but I will keep on learning.'

The focus switched to Saturday's derby, but Sir Alex found himself distracted by an over-sensationalised newspaper claim that Paul Scholes, who had been out of action since the game at Birmingham, was in danger of losing his sight. The manager calmed worried fans by swiftly setting the record straight.

'It's straightforward. I can only tell you what the medical people have said and that is that he has blurred vision and, until that clears, we can't play him. I can't add to that. He has had a scan and nothing has shown up. He definitely has not got a cyst on his eye, I can assure you of that.

'The problem is when people write things like this, that he's going blind, it means I have to respond and I shouldn't really need to. Three years ago they were door-stepping his parents saying he had cancer. God almighty. What kind of journalism are we dealing with nowadays?

'And we have to respond to it. I am answering something that I shouldn't have to. There is nothing there. It is straightforward. He has blurred vision. It doesn't mean to say he is dying. Christ! We don't know how long he is going to be out, but while he has still got blurred vision, I, as a coach, would not pick him anyway.'

And the game?

'Derby games are derby games and over the years when we have faced City they have always had something to prove. That's the danger of it and that's why you have to be 100 per cent. In the last couple of derbies at home we have dominated but missed a lot of chances and finished up with a point, so that tells you a lot about these games.

SATURDAY 14 JANUARY 2006

SCORER:
Van Nistelrooy 76

ATTENDANCE:
47,192

Barclays Premiership
Manchester City 3   Manchester United 1

UNITED: VAN DER SAR, NEVILLE, FERDINAND, SILVESTRE, EVRA (SMITH 46), RONALDO, FLETCHER (SAHA 71), O'SHEA (RICHARDSON 86), GIGGS, ROONEY, VAN NISTELROOY. SUBS NOT USED: HOWARD, BROWN.

Derby disaster and the last thing United wanted. It was a defeat full of implications. Chelsea's next game was forty-eight hours away when they faced bottom club Sunderland, whose chances of pulling off a shock were remote. The Black Cats were far from lucky with only six points won all season. On top of that, Liverpool were now favourites to take over second place having got to within a point of the Reds with two games in hand. Next up for United? Liverpool at Old Trafford!

The Scousers started haunting United at Eastlands when former Anfield favourite Robbie Fowler rubberstamped City's win by scoring their third in the last minute. Before that Trevor Sinclair and Darius Vassell gave the Blues a 2–0 lead by half time, with van Nistelrooy bringing false hope by scoring in the seventy-sixth minute. However, to rub salt into United's wounds, they had played the last half hour without Cristiano Ronaldo, who was sent off after making a spectacular leap towards Andy Cole.

The incident came only moments after United had what appeared to be a justifiable appeal for a free kick turned down when Ronaldo was floored during a break down the right flank. His reaction was to try to win the ball back and although he made no contact with Cole, and replays showed there seemed no malicious intent, the dismissal completed a dismal day.

'You get these reminders from time to time what derby games are all about. We didn't respond to it. I thought our first half was poor. In the second we improved quite a bit in terms of possession of the ball and control of the game, but the sending off was a killer,' said Sir Alex.

'When we got the goal back I felt we had a chance, but we sent all our men up in the last minutes, so it was understandable we might lose that third goal.'

Four days before the Liverpool clash came the FA Cup game against Burton, but as he got ready for the replay, goalkeeper Tim Howard was still reflecting on what might have been. He had watched Saturday's upset from the bench.

'I was chomping at the bit along with some of the other boys. Not because we could do it better, or worse, but it's a team. We feel for the boys who were out there. It wasn't coming off for them and it's not only disappointment you feel when that happens, but frustration because you can't do much about it.'

As far as the replay was concerned he could.

Tim was about to make his fifth start of the season and was confident that United would get through to a fourth-round tie away to Wolves.

'Whether it's a Premiership side or a non-league one, we are supposed to go out there and win. We don't look at them as only being non-league; they gave a good account of themselves and I think they will again tonight, but it's up to us to prove our worth and our strength and beat them. On the day they played pretty well and you have to take your hat off to them. Now they are coming to Old Trafford and, over the years, it has been our backbone. Enormous teams have come here and folded, so we are hoping that happens again.'

WEDNESDAY 18 JANUARY 2006

FA Cup, Third Round Replay
Manchester United 5   Burton Albion 0

UNITED: HOWARD, BARDSLEY, BROWN (NEVILLE 62), PIQUE, SILVESTRE, SOLSKJAER, FLETCHER (GIGGS 62), O'SHEA (FERDINAND 62), RICHARDSON, ROSSI, SAHA. SUBS NOT USED: VAN DER SAR, VAN NISTELROOY.

SCORERS:
Saha 7,
Rossi 23, 90,
Richardson 52,
Giggs 68

ATTENDANCE:
53,564

For 11,000 Burton Albion fans – 5,000 more than the total

attendance at the original game – this was their Utopia. They enjoyed their moment of glory, but Giuseppe Rossi had an even better time and the United youngster ran the show, scoring twice and inspiring his team-mates to their biggest win of the season. With Cristiano Ronaldo and Wayne Rooney both suspended, Sir Alex made just one change to the side that had drawn at Burton's Pirelli Stadium, with Darren Fletcher in for Ritchie Jones who had gone to Antwerp.

Once again, Ole Gunnar Solskjaer was made captain and was back on the Old Trafford pitch for the first time in twenty months, as Louis Saha made a firm bid for a regular starting place by opening the scoring after seven minutes. Rossi got his first as he headed home a Silvestre cross in the twenty-third minute, but the 53,564 crowd, whose presence helped make it a bumper pay day for Burton, had to wait till the death before he completed his brace. In between times, Kieran Richardson scored from a Rossi flick and Giggs volleyed home from a Rossi pass. A shot through a crowded box completed the rout and United were in round four.

'If you had told me twenty months ago that I would captain Man United for my first game back at Old Trafford and that we would win 5–0 in the FA Cup, I would have bitten anyone's hand off,' said a satisfied Solskjaer.

'It doesn't matter who the game was against. I'm at Old Trafford, I played, I played ninety minutes and I really, really enjoyed it. The early goal settled us down and we just tried to play some nice football and there were some great goals out there.'

Sir Alex appeared to have mixed feelings about the result and showed a soft spot for Nigel Clough's side.

'I'm pleased with the performance, but we didn't want it to be a humiliation, which it could have been if we had stepped on the gas. Five-nil is a fantastic scoreline and it proves that we treated the game seriously and it was a good professional performance, but credit to Burton, because it was a positive display by them.

'We have had European teams coming here and many

Premiership teams who have not shown half of the positive attitude Burton showed. I can't remember the last team to play two up here. They usually play one striker, pack the midfield and bore the pants off everybody, but Burton played with their own beliefs and their own system and they did well.'

The result meant United would at least go into the Liverpool game on the back of a win, but with Chelsea beating Sunderland on Wearside as expected, the chances of catching the leaders were looking even more remote. The gap between first and second had widened to sixteen points.

'At the moment it doesn't look as though that is going to happen, but you never know,' was Ryan Giggs' view. 'We've got to concentrate on winning our games and not focus on Chelsea. We need them to slip up three or four times, and we also need a good enough run between now and the end of the season to capitalise on that if it does happen.'

Optimism indeed, especially after that derby result.

Ryan was convinced things would tilt United's way and where better to start than against Liverpool, the form side who were breathing down their neck.

'I don't think it really matters with United–Liverpool games where the teams happen to be in the league, or even what sort of form they are in. These are always massive games and for United fans and players, it's the biggest game there is. No matter what Arsenal or Chelsea do, because of the history, the rivalry and the closeness of the two cities, it's always been that way. Liverpool are full of belief right now thanks to the run they are on. They believe they are going to keep clean sheets and score goals and if you've got that sort of confidence you're going to get results.'

Liverpool had not lost a league game since October, when they went down 2–1 at Fulham two weeks after being hammered 4–1 at home by Chelsea. Since then, a run of eleven wins and a draw had swept them up the table. As for Chelsea, their Saturday game at home to Charlton had ended in a shock 1–1 draw so United – or Liverpool – had a chance to make up some ground on them.

SUNDAY 22 JANUARY 2006

SCORER:
Ferdinand 90
ATTENDANCE:
67,874

Barclays Premiership
Manchester United 1   Liverpool 0

UNITED: VAN DER SAR, NEVILLE, FERDINAND, BROWN, EVRA, RICHARDSON, FLETCHER, O'SHEA (SAHA 46), GIGGS, ROONEY, VAN NISTELROOY. SUBS NOT USED: HOWARD, VIDIC, SILVESTRE, ROSSI.

If a week is a long time in politics, a minute can be an eternity in football. Just ask Liverpool. The Merseysiders had the upper hand for much of a game that both sides had to win, but what had happened in the previous eighty-nine minutes meant nothing as United struck with a goal so late that there was no way back for the visitors.

The clash had provided moments to remember, like Steven Gerrard's bone-crunching challenge on his close pal Wayne Rooney midway through the first half, which could have warranted a sending-off on another occasion. There was Wes Brown's desperate clearance from a Peter Crouch shot destined for the back of the net and van der Sar's super save from the lanky striker. Add to that Djibril Cisse's close-range howler, plus chances for Rooney, Giggs then van Nistelrooy, whose shot shaved a post with ten minutes to go, and a picture emerges. But the closing minute was the defining moment and Rio Ferdinand has cause to remember it more than most.

'We won a corner and, as I was running up the field, Gary Neville said to me, "Go on and get us a goal." I got up into the box as I normally do and the ball came across and it was a good ball from Giggsy. It was a little bit behind me, but I headed it and saw it hit the net. That is the best feeling you can ever imagine. I swear to it. My face said it all. You can't explain it. It is just an unbelievable feeling that you want to be there for you all the time and you want to do it every game.

'That's why forwards have got a great job. My job is brilliant, but for forwards to be able to score goals, and the adulation you get in scoring is fantastic.'

Being engulfed by his team-mates was a fairly new experience for the central defender: 'You don't hear anything clearly. It's just a big "Ahhhh!" It's just noise. It's nothing significant. There are no words that stand out. It is just one big roar, but it's well worth waiting for. I had scored twice before, against Wigan and West Brom, and that was a great feeling, but to score at the Stretford End, against Liverpool, in the last minute … You can't ask for a better story than that.'

'Rio has threatened to score a few times and he took a lot of stick for coming up for corners and not getting any goals,' revealed a jubilant Ryan Giggs.

'It was great to see him score. We have always had players who could come up from the back and score. He had been telling us about this great celebration he had planned, but he forgot all about it. He just ran towards the fans and enjoyed the moment. It was brilliant for Rio, especially scoring the winning goal against Liverpool in the last minute at Old Trafford … it doesn't get any better than that.'

So what about that celebration? Rio explains.

'I don't know. When I got my first goal it came after a long wait, but when it did, especially from a corner, it was good. It kind of got me on the road and it was a great feeling. It was the relief as well and the enjoyment of finally scoring, because I have been here so long and it was a nice way for me to kind of give something back.'

Was it going to be boogying on the byline, grabbing the corner flag and doing an Elvis?

'I was going to do a little dance or something like that, but I think I have matured a bit and I didn't! But the occasion kind of grabs hold of you and you just erupt. All the emotions come out at once and you don't really do anything. We just went bananas and I got a great buzz out of looking into the eyes of a lot of the fans and seeing the enjoyment that they got and that was obviously reflected in the way that I celebrated.'

Captain Neville had his own way of enjoying the win.

On the whistle he ran towards the Scoreboard End screaming

his delight and kissing his shirt badge. The problem was his demonstration appeared to be directed towards the visiting support and the next day, it was that after-match moment that filled the back pages rather than the story of the game itself. Liverpool fans complained, sparking off a media uproar that alerted the FA and, faced with possible punishment, Gary turned to Man United Radio to give his side of the story.

'When you lose a game against Liverpool or Manchester City, you have to take the stick you are going to get walking round the streets. Then, when you win, they have to take a bit, but it doesn't always seem that people accept it when Manchester United players give it out. You accept their support is going to give you stick all afternoon, sing things about you, and I don't have any problem with that. But there should be no problem when the boot is on the other foot and they get a little bit back. That is football and what makes it a great game, because there is passion involved.

'We were delighted with the victory and it had been a long time since we had won a big game like that in the last minute and they are the real sweet ones. We have lost as well, people forget that, four years ago, Danny Murphy scored for Liverpool at Old Trafford with three minutes to go, and we had to see Liverpool's players huddling at the Stretford End. People have short memories.

'I would have celebrated just the same whether I had been captain or not. It is the way I am. I have been like this for twenty-five years and I am not going to change at the age of thirty. It was purely down to the fact that we won the game. We had lost to our local rivals the week before, but a fixture against Liverpool the week after gives you a great opportunity to put things right.'

Gary was later fined £5,000 after losing his appeal against an FA ruling he described as: 'A poor decision, not just for me but for all footballers. Being a robot, devoid of passion and spirit is obviously the way forward for the modern day footballer. "Where is football being taken?" I ask the authorities.'

The Liverpool victory provided the perfect springboard for the second leg against Blackburn, but before Sir Alex could finalise plans for Blackburn's visit to Old Trafford, he was hit by two more setbacks.

John O'Shea had cracked a rib against Liverpool and would be sidelined for a month, while the news about Paul Scholes was worse. His vision problem had not eased and a specialist recommended that he should rest for at least three months. He was ruled out for the remainder of the season.

'We have to take the medical advice and that is to give him a break and hope it settles down and everybody hopes that's the case,' said the manager before assessing United's chances against a Mark Hughes-inspired Rovers.

'It's a semi-final. You have got to expect that a team thinks it's got a chance and they have, because Mark has done a good job there. They are very hard to beat. They're a strong, physical team. In the first game we were the better side, but I don't think that matters when you get to the second leg of a semi-final.'

One thing was certain, whoever got through to the final, things would be different. Wigan Athletic had pulled off the shock of the season by beating Arsenal 2–1 at Highbury in the other semi-final and the game was guaranteed to be an all-northern affair, giving skipper Neville added incentive to get through.

Three days after conquering Liverpool, he was now just ninety minutes away from leading United to a final in the first two months of his captaincy, but he made it clear the players could not bask in Sunday's glory.

'Immediately after a game like that people might think we are euphoric and we are celebrating, but the moment we got into the changing rooms our thoughts switched to tonight and the fact that this is probably as big, if not bigger, than the Liverpool game.

'We have an opportunity to get to a final and we have to win trophies. People will point out that the Carling Cup isn't one of the major trophies, but if we were to pick up a trophy at the end of February, who knows where that would take us by the end of the season? It's important we keep ticking over, keep picking up trophies. We may not be able to win the European Cup this year and the league is looking particularly difficult, but we have to keep winning and this is an opportunity to do that.'

Gary also felt as though there was a point to prove.

'I don't know whether anyone else feels it, people will say it is paranoia, but I just get the feeling there is an undercurrent of dis-respect towards Manchester United. Leading up to the Liverpool game it was all about "Changes in power" and I hear a lot of these phrases mentioned towards Manchester United. We lose a game, our first in two and a half months, and we are slated for it.

'We win against Liverpool on Sunday and the headlines are about me getting an FA ban and being rapped on the knuckles, rather than about us winning the game. At the moment we don't seem to be able to get away from the disrespect being shown towards us. We may not be playing at our greatest level, or be top of the league, but we are still fighting like mad and doing our very best and people should understand where we are trying to get to and what we are doing.

'We don't want praise when we have not done well. We under-stand the criticism when you lose 3–1 at Manchester City, but it seems to be going over the top a little bit in the last year or so and we, the players, are the only ones who can put that right by winning trophies.

'Winning matches is the only thing ultimately that will turn it around. If we win tonight it might silence a few people for a few days, but we have a very difficult game. They have already won at Old Trafford this season and couldn't be in better form.

'We are lifted after the result on Sunday and it does make for a great semi-final. It's well poised at 1–1 and the away goals don't come into it unless it goes to extra-time. We have just got to go and win a football match at Old Trafford and that is something we always feel confident of doing.'

WEDNESDAY 25 JANUARY 2006

Carling Cup, Semi-Final, Second Leg
Manchester United 2   Blackburn Rovers 1

UNITED: VAN DER SAR, NEVILLE, FERDINAND, BROWN, EVRA (SILVESTRE 80), ROONEY, FLETCHER, GIGGS (SMITH 13), RICHARDSON, SAHA, VAN NISTELROOY (VIDIC 86). SUBS NOT USED: HOWARD, ROSSI.

SCORERS:
Van Nistelrooy 8,
Saha 51

ATTENDANCE:
61,637

Sensational Saha strikes again. Another goal from Louis ties things up and books United's place in the final, but what a battle this was. Sir Alex made his intentions clear by again fielding a strong line-up and making three changes to the side that had started the first game. Patrice Evra came in for Mikael Silvestre, Richardson for the suspended Ronaldo, and Ruud van Nistelrooy for Alan Smith.

'Once you get into a semi-final you have to go for it,' he explained. 'There was the year we beat Chelsea in the semi-final and then lost the final to Liverpool; last season we were beaten in the semi-final by Chelsea – when, by the way, we had two penalty kicks turned down, one in each leg, which would have got us through – each round we got stronger and stronger as we got nearer to Cardiff.'

United made the perfect start. Van Nistelrooy, making his first start in the competition, demonstrated his predatory powers after just eight minutes when Ryan Giggs stole the ball from Rovers left-back Michael Gray, found Wayne Rooney, who ran into the box, passed to Ruud and he poked home from close range.

Five minutes later, United's troubles started when Giggs limped off with a hamstring problem; his replacement Alan Smith was booked after a crunching challenge on Robbie Savage; then Rovers scored.

The goal was no classic. A Richardson clearance hit Wes Brown and fell to Steven Reid, whose weak shot somehow beat van der Sar.

Just before half time things got worse when van Nistelrooy had a penalty saved by Brad Friedel after Khizanishvili handled, but it was after the whistle that things really appeared to heat up. An incident between Savage and van Nistelrooy led to Ferdinand having words with the Blackburn midfielder and the two kept the argument going as they entered the tunnel, with players from both sides intervening in a bid to calm things down.

The winner came six minutes into the second half, when Darren Fletcher overpowered Tugay in midfield and found Rooney. He made ground before crossing to Saha, who sweetly volleyed home for his fifth goal in four Carling ties. Cardiff here we come!

'Semi-finals are never meant to be easy. When you look back over the years, our semi-finals have all been difficult ties, some of them have gone to replays, extra-time, things like that and we have scored some late goals. They are never meant to be easy and tonight was exactly like that,' explained Sir Alex, who was now looking forward to his fourth domestic final in three years.

'Rovers make you work and they make the referee work, too. They are a very competitive, argumentative side and you have to compete with that or you're dead. The stats of the match will be quite interesting; off the top of my head I can think of three saves, possibly four, that Brad Friedel has made which were out of this world. He kept them in this match. It was an incredible performance from a goalkeeper.'

As far as the half-time incident was concerned, the Reds boss did an Arsene Wenger!

'I didn't see anything at the break, I must say that. I was just ambling down the touchline trying to think about the points to make at half time, because it's the most important part of the game for me. At the end of the day we managed to get through, but the injury to Ryan was a blow.

'We have seven days left in the transfer window and we are looking very hard, but it isn't easy. There is no point in bringing someone here just for the sake of bringing him. We would want someone who could contribute and who could be part of the squad, because we are suffering with a lack of numbers in midfield.'

Transfer talk occupied the run-up to the Sunday FA Cup tie at Molineux, with Real Madrid's Thomas Gravesen said to be on the wanted list along with Lyon's Mahamadou Diarra, Simao of Benfica, Johann Vogel and Ivan Gattuso from AC Milan, and, of course, Michael Ballack, whose name reared up again, despite the manager's insistence that United were not interested in the Bayern Munich star.

'Ideally we would have liked to have brought in a midfield player on loan, but we have exhausted that part and it's looking very unlikely. We are recalling Ritchie Jones from Antwerp just to give us some back-up, but we would have preferred someone more experienced. We have had bad injury spells in the past; we have just got to get through it.

There was a midfielder in Sir Alex's thoughts as United set off for Wolverhampton. Paul Ince, the former Old Trafford favourite now in the twilight of a colourful career with the Midlands outfit, was about to cross his old boss's path once again.

'Incey? Oh, I'll be having a quiet word with him. We haven't seen much of each other, but I spoke to him a couple of months ago at a charity event. He's a really good character and he won't be fazed by the game, that's for sure. Others may be, but he won't!'

SUNDAY 29 JANUARY 2006

FA Cup, Fourth Round
Wolverhampton Wanderers 0   Manchester United 3

SCORERS:
Richardson 6, 52, Saha 45

UNITED: VAN DER SAR, NEVILLE, VIDIC, BROWN (SMITH 57), SILVESTRE, FERDINAND, RICHARDSON (EVRA 64), PARK, SAHA (FLETCHER 64), ROONEY, VAN NISTELROOY. SUBS NOT USED: HOWARD, BARDSLEY.

ATTENDANCE:
28,333

After Glenn Hoddle's side were overrun and the Reds reached the last sixteen of the FA Cup, there was hope that United were on course for a domestic cup double.

Kieran Richardson stole the spotlight from Louis Saha with United's intentions made abundantly clear as Sir Alex started with all three main strikers in a 4–3–3 formation. It was also a special occasion for Nemanja Vidic, who was making his full debut, alongside Wes Brown, with Rio Ferdinand patching up the midfield and

Ji-sung Park returned following his knee injury.

United had another flying start, with Richardson scoring after six minutes from a Saha cross and with the Frenchman adding the second just before half time as he fired home a powerful low shot from Vidic's precise long-ball. Wolves had little to offer and, seven minutes into the second half, the contest was over when Richardson got his second, heading home van Nistelrooy's cross.

'After watching videos of their last three games against Luton, Millwall and Plymouth, I expected a difficult game, but we got the goals at the right time,' was Sir Alex's immediate after-match reaction.

'Our counter-attack play at times was very good. Wolverhampton had their moments and when the third goal went in I thought we got a bit slack and could have been punished for it, but they probably felt they were in control.'

Back-to-back starts for Saha brought a response from Louis.

'It's great to be back in a team that is playing better. I'm happy with my own form. Scoring goals is the main thing for a striker, and I just needed games to feel sharper, so everything is coming together.'

With a Premiership return to Blackburn three days after the Wolves win and two after United were drawn against Liverpool at Anfield in the next round, the softly spoken Frenchman wanted to make it three in a row, but there was added reason to try to stay in the side, as the week would end with Fulham, his former club, coming to Old Trafford.

'If Brad Friedel plays the way he normally does against us, it's going to be a very tight game,' Sir Alex forecast as United prepared to hit the road again.

WEDNESDAY 1 FEBRUARY 2006

Barclays Premiership
Blackburn Rovers 4   Manchester United 3

UNITED: VAN DER SAR, NEVILLE, VIDIC, BROWN (SILVESTRE 76), EVRA, RICHARDSON
(VAN NISTELROOY 54), FLETCHER (PARK 54), FERDINAND, RONALDO, ROONEY, SAHA.
SUBS NOT USED: HOWARD, PIQUE.

SCORERS:
Saha 37,
Van Nistelrooy 63,
65

ATTENDANCE:
25,484

Just when it looked safe to go back in the water, along came Blackburn and, on a night Chelsea dropped two points at Aston Villa, United let all three go at Ewood Park! Rovers' revenge was sweet, but it was sour for the Reds to swallow with the home side doing a Premiership double over United in spite of a spirited second-half fightback.

Four goals in ten minutes, two of them from David Bentley, did the damage and from then on United were swimming against the tide. Rovers took the lead in the thirty-fifth minute, Saha equalised two minutes later as he tapped home the remnants of a Rooney rocket that had been stopped by Friedel, then Bentley struck again on forty-one minutes and a Lucas Neill penalty on the stroke of half time made it 3–1.

It looked all over when Bentley completed his hat-trick in the fifty-sixth minute, but an inspired comeback, with substitute Ruud van Nistelrooy scoring twice, at least made a fight of it. The game ended bitterly with Rio Ferdinand sent off after colliding with who else but Robbie Savage and Sir Alex claiming: 'I will need to see the video to be fair, but Rio says he never touched him, so we will find that out later.'

Things might have been worse, but Liverpool threw away the chance of overhauling United by drawing 1–1 at home to Birmingham, making it only too clear that the race for second place was going to be tough.

'I suppose it was an incredible spectacle with goals and excitement, but we've thrown it away,' was the manager's verdict. 'It was one of our best performances in ages in terms of possession of the ball and dominating, but we were 3–1 down at half time. It was amazing. That's football. The first goal the boy came in for a rebound off Edwin van der Sar's great save, the second was a complete mix-up between Edwin and Rio and the third one was going nowhere. The boy mishit it and the linesman gave a penalty when it hit Wes Brown's arm. It was a harsh decision.'

Two-goal van Nistelrooy also found defeat hard to take.

'It's crazy really. Look at every goal they scored? The fourth was a good one, but the others were presents. We had all the play and that was the crazy thing because they didn't get one chance yet they scored three goals and I have never played in a game like this. Everything went bad in one half, so hopefully that's it now for the rest of the season.

'At half time we said that if we could get a goal we would be back in it and even when it went 4–1 we still came into the game. We couldn't push more when we wanted and when you concede four it's a difficult game. After I scored twice with twenty minutes to go, we felt that we still had a chance and that it was game on. We proved we can score goals from nothing and it gave us hope. It's a disappointing night, not a bad performance, but mistakes have cost us and that is a sore thing. Now we have to start another run against Fulham at home.'

Ferdinand's midweek dismissal meant that the England defender-cum-United-midfielder would miss the Fulham game and, on the morning before that encounter, Cristiano Ronaldo learned that he would be sitting out the next European fixture after being handed a one-match ban by UEFA for the way he had reacted to abuse from the Benfica fans in Lisbon.

'What are players supposed to do?' asked Sir Alex. 'I think it's time the authorities started to take into consideration the abuse they have to take from fans. We get a sample of that when someone who has joined us plays against his old club.'

It wasn't quite the Rooney treatment for Louis Saha as he stepped out to face his old club, but the Fulham fans did make their feelings known to the forward who had left Craven Cottage to move to Old Trafford.

Saha's goal run had earned him a fourth successive start and he intended to make the most of it: 'It's a great opportunity to put things together in the Premiership. We missed a chance because Chelsea drew the other night, but we know this is going to be a tough game because every time we play against Fulham it's difficult. I have some great memories of my time at Fulham and still speak to some of my old team-mates on the phone. It was a great family club and I really enjoyed it there, but it would be nice to score against them at Old Trafford.'

SATURDAY 4 FEBRUARY 2006

Barclays Premiership
Manchester United 4   Fulham 2

UNITED: VAN DER SAR, NEVILLE (VIDIC 69), BROWN, SILVESTRE, EVRA (BARDSLEY 81), RONALDO, SMITH, RICHARDSON, PARK (ROONEY 69), SAHA, VAN NISTELROOY. SUBS NOT USED: FLETCHER, STEELE.

SCORERS:
Park 6,
Ronaldo 14, 86,
Saha 23

ATTENDANCE:
67,844

Cristiano Ronaldo showed just how much that Euro-ban had affected him with two strikes in another multi-goal game, although this time the Reds came out on top. It was the perfect response to Wednesday's setback with Ji-sung Park setting things rolling in the sixth minute and Louis Saha also getting his wish by netting a home goal against his old club.

Five goals in the first half, plus a sending off – Fulham boss Chris Coleman red-carded for persisting with his claim that Saha was offside when he scored – 67,844 fans could justifiably claim to be disappointed that the second forty-five minutes produced only one.

Brian McBride and Heidar Helguson scored to help Fulham make a game of it, but when Ronaldo popped up to force home the final goal, after Antti Niemi had brilliantly saved a van Nistelrooy shot, it was all over.

'I expected them to attack us and they did. I have watched them playing against Wigan and Tottenham away from home and they played superbly but didn't win and today they will be saying exactly the same. Played well, didn't win.'

The win meant United had taken fifty-one points from twenty-five games, a better showing than in five of Sir Alex's eight title-winning seasons. No wonder the United boss felt it was time to hand out a few accolades.

'I am really pleased with my players because seventeen games in two months is a phenomenal display of human resource and courage. To play so many in such a short time and get the results we have got; we have had to change teams because of injuries, at one point we had eight players missing, but you have to give credit to the players and to our staff for preparing properly.'

Chelsea were still running away with the league – having beaten Liverpool 2–0 at Stamford Bridge the day after the Fulham game – and while the result did United one favour, by pegging back the Merseysiders, the gap between first and second was still maintained. Jose Mourinho had caused a bit of a stir by predicting that the race was over and that Chelsea would be champions by 9 April. As he laid out his plans for the trip to Portsmouth, Sir Alex was asked for his response.

'It's possible. But as long as you have some games of football to play anything is also possible. I think Jose toys with you journalists a bit and he enjoys it. It's in his nature and we have come to realise that, but his team could do it with the consistency they have shown.

'As for tomorrow, strange as it may seem, we have a clean bill of health. No injuries from last week, the only one we are waiting to come back is John O'Shea and he'll be training with us next week. He may not be ready to play, but at least he will be on the way back. The two long-term ones, Gaby and Quinton, are missing obviously, but it's good. It gives me problems; with all the attacking options, we just have to create the right balance.'

SATURDAY 11 FEBRUARY 2006

Barclays Premiership

Portsmouth 1   Manchester United 3

UNITED: VAN DER SAR (HOWARD 46), BROWN, FERDINAND, VIDIC, SILVESTRE, RONALDO, FLETCHER, GIGGS (SMITH 46), PARK, ROONEY (SAHA 82), VAN NISTELROOY. SUBS NOT USED: EVRA, RICHARDSON.

SCORERS:
Van Nistelrooy 17,
Ronaldo 38, 45

ATTENDANCE:
20,206

If United needed a boost before this 5.15 p.m. kick-off, it came with the news that Jose Mourinho's 9 April party had been put on hold because Chelsea had lost 3–0 at Middlesbrough. Perhaps that October upset at The Riverside was no fluke after all! So, as the Premiership leaders made their way home, United made sure that if they were following the action from Fratton Park, they would have something else to spoil their weekend.

Ruud van Nistelrooy scored the first in the seventeenth minute with Cristiano Ronaldo putting United firmly in control by adding two more before half time. His first was a sensational strike which came after a chest down by van Nistelrooy. Ruud laid the ball perfectly into Ronaldo's path with the Portuguese youngster hitting a ferocious 25 yard volley which ripped past Pompey 'keeper Dean Kiely and threatened to tear its way through the net. (The goal would later top the fans' poll in the End of Season Awards as best of the campaign.)

His second was less spectacular but arguably of greater value, as it gave United a 3–0 cushion, with Ronaldo forcing the ball home from just inside the penalty area after running onto a Rooney pass. Even when Tim Howard replaced the injured Edwin van der Sar after the break the pattern did not change, with Pompey forced to wait until the eighty-seventh minute before Matthew Taylor scored their goal.

Van Nistelrooy's goal took him closer to a major milestone. He had scored 148 times in 207 United appearances and was just two strikes away from joining legendary figures like Sir Bobby Charlton, Denis Law, Jack Rowley, George Best and Joe Spence as the only other Old

Trafford stars to have scored 150 times for the club.

With Saturday's FA Cup tie at Liverpool coming up, Ruud confessed that there would be no better way of joining the 150 club than by putting his side in the quarter-finals with a brace at Anfield.

'The game itself is huge. Manchester United versus Liverpool at Anfield in an FA Cup tie is very special. To be able to do well in a game like that would be more than special. The object is to win and go to the next round. For me, I want to play well and I would love to score. That would be fantastic. We have had some good results there, but I have yet to score at Anfield and that would be great to do it on Saturday. If I could get two, well!

'Personal records are a proud thing, but I want to win things as well. I am proud of what I have achieved at United. It has been five fantastic years and I hope this season will bring silverware again. When I look back on the finals I have played in and the title I was part of, that's what it is all about as a footballer playing for United.

'Yes, when I joined in 2001 they had won something like seven out of the last ten Premiership titles. They had won the Champions League in 1999 and the Treble. The expectations for everyone then, and I suppose myself, was that United were going to win another eight titles in ten years. But football is not as simple as that. We are in a situation now where we are improving. Anyone who sees these young players now and the mix we are trying to create must see and understand that things are coming on. Hopefully with that the future will be great and I am looking forward to that.'

The win over Pompey meant that United gained three points on Chelsea for only the second time in the season, and still trailed by fifteen points with a game in hand, but for Ruud the race was still on.

'Finishing second would mean automatic qualification for next season's Champions League, when we can do something about it again. But I am not even thinking of second yet. I can't get the words out of my mouth to not still go for the title because it is not over. That's why we will always still go for it. We will keep doing that, because it is not finished yet.

'Winning matches, like an FA Cup tie at Anfield and getting

silverware in Cardiff against Wigan, will all help to build this young squad into a great squad in the future. We are building something at United. It is a team that can be the best again if we continue the progress we are making.'

It was passionate stuff from the Dutchman.

Gary Neville was also reaching a milestone. The Liverpool game was on his thirty-first birthday, but it turned out to be one he would rather forget.

SATURDAY 18 FEBRUARY 2006

FA Cup, Fifth Round
Liverpool 1   Manchester United 0

Attendance:
44,039

UNITED: VAN DER SAR; NEVILLE, BROWN, VIDIC, SILVESTRE (SAHA 46), FLETCHER (SMITH 77 (PARK 90)), GIGGS, RICHARDSON, RONALDO, ROONEY, VAN NISTELROOY. SUBS NOT USED: HOWARD, PIQUE.

One goal, one miss and one terrible moment. That tells the story of United's exit from the FA Cup. The goal came after nineteen minutes, scored by Liverpool's beanpole striker Peter Crouch, and was enough to give the Merseysiders their first FA Cup win over United for eighty-five years.

With Rio Ferdinand missing, after picking up a slight hamstring problem in training, Nemanja Vidic was drafted in for an Anfield baptism of fire as birthday boy Neville ran a gauntlet of abuse throughout the afternoon.

Ruud van Nistelrooy thought he had made it to 149, only to have his equaliser rubbed out by an offside flag. Saha, brought on for Silvestre in the second half, had a powerful header scraped off the line before seeing what he thought was an equaliser also disallowed for offside, then a terrific drive from Ryan Giggs went the wrong side of the crossbar.

However, this game will be remembered for one thing only: the horrific injury suffered by Alan Smith in the closing minutes. Liverpool were awarded a free kick and, as John Arne Riise prepared to take it, Ryan Giggs formed part of the barrier.

'I was in the wall with Smudger and they just tapped the free kick to the side and he went out to block it, bravely, like he does and he just caught his foot in the grass. I didn't actually see what happened next because the game played on, but as soon as I went over to see him I knew it was a bad one.'

Smith's foot had caught in the turf and, as his momentum carried him forward, his leg snapped above the ankle. He sat motionless. As Ruud van Nistelrooy called to the bench in horror, and Edwin van der Sar ran to help, Wes Brown knelt down to comfort his team-mate.

'It was horrible. At first Alan was shouting to me and I could see he was in pain, but I thought he had cramp and I was going over to sort it out. Then I saw his ankle. I just grabbed hold of him and I didn't want him to lie down just in case something moved, so I tried to hold him there and started to shout to the referee.

'Alan went grey, then white, and I kept saying, "Relax you'll be fine."

'Smudger' Smith was stretchered off, seven minutes of stoppage time were played and United were out of the cup. However, few in the camp were thinking about the result.

'When you are drawn away from home in a cup-tie like that it can go either way. They are not an easy side to play against. It's probably not the best Liverpool team of all time, but it is certainly one of the hardest to play against. It doesn't say you are a bad team because you get knocked out in an FA Cup-tie, because one year we got knocked out by West Ham at home when everyone expected us to win. We got knocked out against Middlesbrough when everybody thought we would get through, so that is the way it is,' was how Sir Alex summed up defeat, but his main concern was the welfare of his player.

'At the time it seemed so innocuous. There was no one near him really, but I knew it was bad. When they took him off he was covered, of course, but when I went into the Liverpool treatment room with Bobby to see him. It was ...

'You knew it was bad because of the reaction of van der Sar first of all then, van Nistelrooy and Wes Brown, Gary Neville. You knew it was bad, the bone all ... jeez. It's the worst I've ever seen, but he was so calm. He just put his hand up to tell us he was injured. Alan handled it fantastically well. It was a really bad injury and the Liverpool medical staff did a great job. They were great.'

Not so certain factions of the Anfield support, though. After Smith went down, some Liverpool fans on The Kop burst into an unsavoury song about the incident, with their chants silenced only when the majority of supporters realised the severity of the injury. To make matters worse, as the midfielder was being taken to hospital, reports came in to suggest that stones had been thrown at the ambulance.

With the weekend over Liverpool Football Club reacted, with Sir Alex happy to accept their apologies.

'It was terrible what the Liverpool supporters did, but I was delighted that Liverpool came out and criticised them because they don't always do that. But they knew the seriousness of it. That was bad and I would take it that Manchester United supporters would never behave like that to an opponent, and I have to say ninety per cent of the Liverpool fans applauded Alan off the field. It just shows you that the true element of football supporters are good because they want to see football played the right way, but there is also that bad element.

'We have got one or two who have let us down from time to time, that you don't want to see. It happens right across the country. Now, as far as Alan is concerned, we think it is a seven-month job, so we should have him back in September.'

As for Alan, the joker in United's pack, his reaction to the injury was typical of the man: 'I felt my leg go from under me as I went to block the free kick. When I looked down, the leg was lying one way and my ankle was pointing towards Hong Kong, so I knew I was in serious trouble! But the doctors are being very positive. I've had the operation and now it's a question of starting on the road back.'

Ryan Giggs is looking forward to the day. 'Just seeing the courage of Smudger, I have no doubt that he will be back soon and back to normal ... the Smudger that everyone loves and who everyone has come to love at the club.'

CHAPTER SEVEN

A Cardiff cup of joy and the toast is 'Smudger'

There was a sharp contrast to the approach taken by the Carling Cup finalists when the countdown to the big day began.

Understandably, Wigan Athletic saw the trip to Cardiff as a unique occasion. It was the first time the club had reached a major final and, after a successful start to life in the Premiership, it provided the club with the perfect opportunity to reward supporters with a great day out at the Millennium Stadium. It also presented Paul Jewell and his players with a rare chance to enjoy a taste of the big time. On Monday 20 February, six days ahead of the game, the doors to the JJB Stadium were thrown open and television, radio and newspaper journalists poured through. They had a field day, as the manager and players obliged.

As for United, they announced it would be business as usual. There would be the normal Friday press conference at Carrington, but because it was a final, Gary Neville would be joining the manager to face the mass media. The knockers loved it. They turned on the Reds, accusing the club of treating the game with contempt, of taking it too lightly, but as will be revealed later, they were way off the mark. Sir Alex's week began with a check on the fitness of Alan Smith.

'The operation has been very successful. It was a bad one, of course, it was terrible, but he has a lot of things in his favour: his courage and his age. He is only twenty-five and there is absolutely no question he can come back from that. Maybe it is a longer one than normal for a broken leg, there were complications with the ankle joint, but we have plated the fibula and in six to seven months he should be back.

'When I went to see him, he was so philosophical about it. He just said "It's football" and that is very commendable. People with character like that give themselves a better chance than normal people.'

He also used the early part of the week to relax in front of his television and follow the progress of the Premiership clubs who had made it to the knock-out phase of the Champions League. In the first leg games, Arsenal had proved the surprise package, beating Real Madrid in the Bernabeu, Chelsea had been stunned by a 2–1 home defeat at the hands of Barcelona, while Benfica, who had proved part of United's downfall, had taken a 1–0 lead over Liverpool after the game in Lisbon.

Had Sir Alex looked on in envy?

'When you have been in football as long as I have, you have to accept that disappointments happen. When I was with Aberdeen, we went out at an unlikely stage and I remember saying to the players, "You better get used to *Coronation Street*," because Wednesday nights are important in European football. I watched the games this week and enjoyed them. I thought it was terrific viewing and at least it took away the threat of a heart attack because I wasn't involved. There is always something to be learned by watching football and I enjoyed it because it reminded me of the level we need to get to and, as in the case of Arsenal, that anything can happen in a game. 'Everybody had written them off, but they went to Real Madrid with one or two players missing from their strongest side and beat the most successful club in the history of the European Cup 1–0. These are all positives for us.'

By the time Friday arrived, the manager made it clear he would be taking nothing for granted. He was in charge of the clear favourites, but he was also fully aware that non-United football fans would be backing the underdogs. There was no room for error.

'As we have always experienced, cup finals are cup finals and they won't ever change. You have to perform. It's a big occasion for us in the sense that Wigan are bringing a bit of romance to it. What they have achieved over the years from where they started in 1977 coming into the league, the drive of Dave Whelan and Paul Jewell the manager have made them an outstanding team this year. Quite rightly the whole country will be behind them and I think that's good.

'The only way you can enjoy a cup final is to win it. When you lose it's felt very deeply among all the players. They are all sick and you can see what it means in their faces. They will not be wanting that on Sunday.'

Gary Neville was swift to point out that United had been in finals before as favourites and that it had all gone wrong.

'I remember losing my first cup final against Everton in my first season and the week before we had lost the league. It does hurt you, so you have to take every cup final as if it's going to be your last because you just don't know.

'We have young lads in the side who already have the experience of losing last year against Arsenal and that just shows you what can happen. We played very well that day, but couldn't score. You have to be ruthless and clinical and take your chances when they come and hopefully we will show the experience we learned in this game. It's not unusual when we play for us to be favourites and for the rest of the country to want us to lose. It's something we have to put up with.

'Wigan have had a great season and when they were at Old Trafford, I liked the way they played the game. They came and had a right go. They didn't sit back and defend and they'll do the same again on Sunday, to make it very difficult for us.'

Sir Alex revealed that one member of the United squad would not be making the trip to south Wales: 'Alan Smith won't be travelling with us. He felt that the recuperation has to go on and he is going to stay at home, but I can be positive about the future. The players will be thinking about Alan because he showed a courage that went to another level. It was amazing to handle it the way that he did.'

'We want to win it for Alan,' added Gary. 'And we want to win it for the club. I'm sure the lads will be ringing him as soon as the game is over, come what may. He should be with us and it's sad for us that he isn't. We are all disappointed for him and like the boss said, he has a really good character and is a solid lad. He has a great attitude and I am sure he will be back next season playing for us. I've spoken to him and wished him all the best and he wished us the same. I just hope we can win because he will have been part of it.'

Would winning make up for other disappointments?

'Going out of Europe is not something we're happy about. We want to put that right next season. When we see the other teams playing in the great stadiums, great games. We have been used to that and it's where we want to get back to as quickly as possible.

'That's where we believe we should be and we have had a really good run in the Champions League over the past nine years where we have got to the quarter-finals virtually every year, so it's strange for us in that sense. We aren't happy about what's happened in the Champions League this season, but we can't do anything about it now, we have to concentrate on the games in front of us and look forward to next season.

'The boss always says we set out every season to win a trophy and there are only four to be won. It's impossible for you to win them all every season. But there are also teams who will not even get the chance to win anything. We have an opportunity on Sunday to go and win a trophy and we shouldn't take that lightly. In the last couple of weeks, when I have been interviewed about this game, it seems to have been approached in a negative way, but we are looking at it in a positive way, about Manchester United reaching a cup final.'

Had going out of the FA Cup had any lasting effect?

'You don't come in every day and sense frustration and hurt. At times, if we lose, you can sense the disappointment, but the fact we have game after game, you don't have much time to feel down. You have to pick yourself up and get yourself ready for the next game and that is always the thought, not just at this club, but at every club, because you are playing so regularly.'

In its many guises, the Football League Cup has eluded United over the years. Sunday would be their sixth appearance in its final, but compared to achievements in other competitions, the success rate fell well short. Five finals played, one won. On top of that, Sir Alex found himself regularly criticised for using the competition as a launching pad for young players, something which at times had led to a premature exit from the competition. This was a pattern followed by other clubs, but the manager claimed that rule changes were now allowing a different approach.

'When the Champions League introduced the group stages in 1994, our squad was nothing like it is nowadays as far as numbers are concerned. There was no way we could play our strongest team in the early stages of the League Cup. That was when we started to introduce the young kids.

'We brought them in against Port Vale and a lot of people objected to it. They even raised it in parliament. Some MP wanted us banned from football and wanted us fined by the FA because I played what he claimed was a weakened team. Even John Rudge, the Port Vale manager, was angry with me, but we beat them 2–1 and Paul Scholes got both our goals. It's become one of those matches where everybody says "I was there". There must have been three million at that game!

'Everybody reckons they saw Beckham make his debut, Scholesy get his goals, Nicky Butt, Gary Neville, Keith Gillespie, but that was the origin of clubs starting to play their fringe players in the League Cup when they were in Europe. We got the bad publicity out of it with everybody saying we didn't care about the competition. In a way it wasn't our biggest priority and, of course, it still isn't today, but that has changed. If you look at the last three or four years, we have done well in the League Cup. When you are in Europe you get in later and before you know it you are in the semi-final.'

Not the biggest priority, but a realistic chance of lifting silverware this season. Would that satisfy Sir Alex?

'Winning one trophy is good. No matter what it is and you have

Another milestone: Ruud van Nistelrooy scores his 150th United goal to help United to a crucial 2–1 victory at Bolton on 1 April. It had taken him just 214 games to reach this figure, which only seven others have done before.

Ji-sung Park scores United's second in their emphatic 2–0 win over Arsenal, on an occasion when the club celebrated fifty years since the Busby Babes won their first title and the gap behind Chelsea was now just seven points.

Mikael Silvestre had one of his best games of the season against Arsenal, including setting up Wayne Rooney for the first goal, and shutting out the Gunners' attack.

Edwin van der Sar is distraught to have conceded a goal against Spurs – no surprise from a man who kept twenty-five clean sheets in fifty-one appearances. United still won to ensure they went to Stamford Bridge with the chance of keeping the title race alive.

Paulo Ferreira's tackle on Wayne Rooney, during which Wayne fell and broke his metatarsal. The injury overshadowed Chelsea's clinching of the Premiership title with a 3–0 victory.

Ryan Giggs is handed the Players' Player of the Year trophy by Sir Alex Ferguson in the first Players' Awards Dinner, on 3 May. It was just reward for the ever-green star, who is now third in the all-time list of most appearances for United.

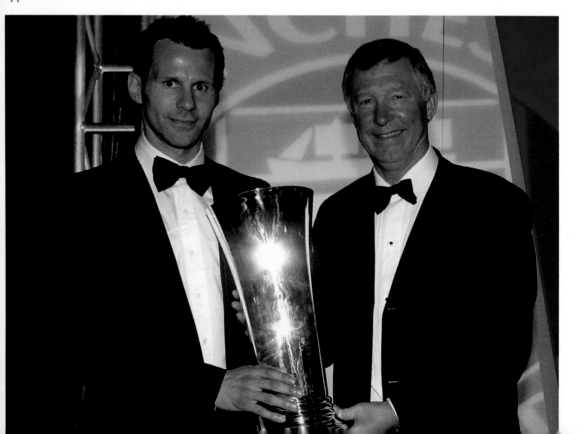

Paul Scholes put in a surprise appearance in the last game of the season against Charlton, having been out of action since December with eye trouble.

Sir Alex Ferguson congratulates Alan Smith at the end of the game. The season had ended with a trophy and United in second place with an impressive 83 points – but already he was looking to go one better in 2006–07: 'I think it could be next year.'

to take that as a successful season, because there are big clubs who are not going to win anything this year. It isn't easy in our league. We had a great spell in the nineties, but from the moment we won the European Cup there was a catch-up by all clubs, realising that a British team could do that. It was great for British football, but it also created a far bigger demand from other clubs to do the same and we are facing stiffer opposition now.'

As the party prepared for the journey to the team hotel, Gary Neville realised he was two days away from reaching a dream to collect his first trophy as club captain.

'You dream a lot as a kid, especially growing up as a Manchester United fan. You go to that stadium and believe anything is possible. On Sunday there is a possibility that could happen, but I am more interested that we win for the club and for the players, because we know winning trophies does give great confidence and that's what we hope Sunday will bring for us.

'I went to finals as a youngster watching United and one of the reasons you fall in love with the club is because of moments like that. I know that out of the 35–40,000 fans who travel to Cardiff, there'll be a large number of kids and we have to make them dream and give them a performance they can be proud of.'

Did that add to the responsibility?

'It does. But it's one I have always been aware of when I have played in cup finals down the years for United.'

The captain's challenge would come once the game got underway, but on the morning of the final, the manager had the task of naming the side to face Wigan: eleven starters five substitutes.

'It's terrible leaving someone out of a final. The worst decision I have taken without question was leaving Bryan Robson out of my substitutes in 1994. That was my hardest one, because there was a guy who deserved to play. He was leaving the club, he was going to become a manager and had his future mapped out in a different direction. I had to look after the players who would be with me the following year, but I should have played Bryan.

'I made a mistake with that, but that is the kind of thing you have to do at this club. You have to make hard decisions and not be afraid to make them. You cannot let the personality or the emotion get to you in that way. At the end of the day, you have to be hard headed enough to make the tough decision.'

Without Robson, United had won the FA Cup in 1994, completing the Double for the first time. Surely that justified the decision?

'Yes, I know but … I made Brian McClair a sub and quite rightly, but I also put Lee Sharpe there as well, just because he had a left foot and if anything had happened on the left-hand side we could have played him there, but Bryan didn't deserve it.'

John O'Shea was worried he might be one of those who would miss the game.

'I got up fairly early and didn't know if I was going to be in the team because I had only just come back from that rib injury. Sometimes you get a feeling during training sessions that you might be playing, but I still didn't know. It was two hours beforehand and the manager was doing his team talk when I found out I had been picked to play in midfield with Giggsy.'

Not so Darren Fletcher, who had started every round except the opener against Barnet.

'It's hard to take when the manager names the team and you aren't in it, but obviously you did your part to get them there. You haven't been selected, but the manager picks the team he feels is best and which is going to win the game. You aren't selected and you're disappointed, but you still wish the rest of your team-mates the best of luck and desperately hope they win it.'

The other surprise was that Louis Saha had been preferred to leading scorer Ruud van Nistelrooy. After the warm-up, the Dutchman would take his place on the bench as one of the substitutes.

SUNDAY 26 FEBRUARY 2006

Carling Cup Final
Manchester United 4   Wigan Athletic 0

UNITED: VAN DER SAR, NEVILLE, FERDINAND, BROWN (VIDIC 83), SILVESTRE (EVRA 83), RONALDO (RICHARDSON 74), O'SHEA, GIGGS, PARK, ROONEY, SAHA. SUBS NOT USED: HOWARD, VAN NISTELROOY.

SCORERS:
Rooney 33, 61,
Saha 55,
Ronaldo 59

ATTENDANCE:
66,866

This was not the one-sided affair the scoreline suggests, as plucky Wigan fought all the way, but in the end United's superior skill carried them through, with Sir Alex collecting the twenty-fifth trophy of his Old Trafford career.

Latics were hit not just by United's second-half avalanche, which produced three goals in an amazing six-minute spell, but by the cruellest of blows when goalkeeper Mike Pollitt was forced to limp off after hardly touching the ball. He pulled a hamstring during the opening exchanges and somehow managed to survive until the thirteenth minute before John Filan replaced him.

With the stadium roof closed and United defending the south end where the majority of their support was, the atmosphere was electrifying. This was Greater Manchester's first final, as two clubs from within the new county boundaries laid down in the early seventies collided: the Davids of Wigan against the Goliaths from Old Trafford and it was left to the underdogs to sling the first stone.

Gary Teale sprinted down the right and crossed perfectly. Henri Camara ran in, but the striker could only head over. United struck back with an identical move. This time Gary Neville crossed, Wayne Rooney met the ball perfectly only to see his effort hit the angle of crossbar and post and Pollitt injuring himself in his bid to keep United out.

Rooney was in rampaging mood and, six minutes after Wigan had changed 'keepers, charged down the right leaving defenders in his wake before passing to an unmarked Ronaldo who rushed his shot, miscued, and saw the ball spin harmlessly away.

United began to dominate midfield and, with thirty-three

minutes gone, Rooney struck, seizing his opportunity as Pascal Chimbonda and Arjen de Zeeuw got themselves in a tangle and the Reds led 1–0.

Wigan would not lie down and, as half time approached, Jason Roberts powered his way past Rio Ferdinand and Gary Neville, but failed to finish a fine move. It was up to striking partner Camara to cause the biggest scare six minutes after the restart with a tremendous shot that had van der Sar at full stretch.

The shock spurred United. With ten minutes of the second half gone, Neville was at the heart of another attack, his right-wing cross scrambled home at the second attempt by Saha for his sixth goal of the cup run. Rooney then forced Stephane Henchoz into a mistake, found Saha and Louis laid on the final pass for Ronaldo to make it 3–0 with fifty-nine minutes of the game played. Within two minutes, three became four when Rio Ferdinand headed down and Rooney grabbed his second.

The Wigan dream was over, but skipper Neville's had come true.

Delight filled one half of the stadium, despair the other, as Wigan's players collapsed in tears. United commiserated, congratulating their opponents on a spirited fight as shirts were swapped and handshakes were exchanged. The Reds bathed in the adulation of the masses as the presentation rostrum was being assembled, but before going up to collect the trophy, the players gathered together. Kit man Albert Morgan and other members of the backroom staff handed out white T-shirts which were hurriedly put on.

Each bore the words: 'For You Smudger'.

'We knew he would be watching the game on television and we hope it spurs him on and I'm sure it will,' said Ryan Giggs. 'That was just a great testament to Smudger's bravery and we all hope he'll be back soon. He has been a big part of the season and is going through a difficult time and we just hope it helps in his recovery and rehabilitation. I thought it was a great touch because even though we were celebrating we were still thinking of a player who, but for the injury, would probably have been playing in the final.'

Ryan reckoned the final was a game United dare not lose.

'That's the pressure you have to handle when you play for Man United and I hope the players in that dressing room thrive on it after winning this trophy and we can go on to win more. I thought Wayne and Louis were a handful today, but it was a real team effort; Wes and Rio were magnificent at the back in the way they handled the threat of Roberts and Camara.'

United had collected another trophy, but for Gary Neville it was a first. 'For somebody who's grown up supporting Manchester United, that was as good as it gets. It couldn't get any better in that respect, but I am aware that the bigger trophies are what this club is about. When Roy and Steve Bruce and Bryan Robson used to lift them, it probably gave me an even bigger buzz because they were such massive trophies. I just hope we can put out a team that has the confidence to go on and challenge for championships and European Cups.

'I have lifted trophies before when I captained the lower teams, but this is better than all the rest because the others were things like youth team trophies or reserve leagues and things like that. In terms of importance this is the biggest as far as I am concerned because it is the only time I have done it with the first team.

'It's also the trophy that has eluded me as a player. I have never won the League Cup, so it was an important match for us. We knew it was important. We had to finish the season with silverware. People will always show sarcasm and a cynical attitude towards the club for winning the League Cup, but it is obvious to everybody that this team is growing. It's gone through some transition over the last couple of years. The people who watch the club know that we are going in the right direction.'

Wes Brown looked down proudly at the medal now hanging around his neck.

'This was the only medal I hadn't got. It was disappointing when we lost to Liverpool three years ago, so it was brilliant today. We knew it was going to be a tough game; they have two strong lads up front, but we competed with them. To be fair, they kept going and even when it was 4–0 they didn't stop, so all credit to them. This is a big win for us and one we needed. We didn't want to go three years without a trophy, but it's in there now and the lads are all lifting their heads up and we're all happy.

'We were glad to get here. It's a special occasion, a cup final. None of us looked upon it as "just the Carling Cup final". To us it's a final. Win a medal. Win a trophy and it all tallies up. We knew the only way we could do that was by playing well and I think we did.

'People go on about it being the third best trophy and all that sort of thing. To us it doesn't matter, it's another trophy. Everybody said we were going to go out there and batter Wigan, but they have done brilliantly this season and we still had to show them what we can do. It was a big scoreline, but at the same time it was a tough game and confidence grew. We all knew what we could do and everybody was playing well. That happens. You start to play and you score great goals.'

Sir Alex also enjoyed the moment: 'Finals are finals and you want to win them and today it was marvellous. Both sets of fans had a great day out; it was a good attacking game from both teams and fortunately we got the goals that mattered. It doesn't matter if it's the World Tiddlywinks Championship … you put it on in Cardiff with that roof closed and 45,000 United fans inside and you have got an atmosphere.

'That is the whole thing about a final in Cardiff, I think it is a great venue. The whole bowl thing with the roof closed, it is fantastic. Everybody loved the day and they loved it because we won. It might have been that little more special because it was against Wigan and they are a local team so there was a bit of a derby about it.'

Why had van Nistelrooy been left out?

'As far as that was concerned it was straightforward. Louis had played all the way through and there was no way he wasn't going to play in the final. People will try to make something of it, but it was a straightforward situation. Louis deserved to play, he had scored five goals on the way to the final and if he hadn't been injured at the time of the Barnet game he would have played in that round, too.

If I had played Ruud and not Louis that would have been worse.'

Did Louis expect to play? Was he worried his goals from the previous rounds might count for nothing? They were questions the Frenchman was happy to answer. 'No. Not definitely, no one is guaranteed to play. This is a big club with big players, so you have to work hard in training to show that you can do something at the weekend. Because I had been playing OK in the previous games, it didn't mean I was going to continue to play.

'I learned I was playing like everyone else, when the team was decided about two hours before. We went in for the pre-match meal and I was very happy with that. While I wouldn't have been happy to be on the bench, it was a good opportunity to show my ability and, having got there, I was happy like everyone else on the pitch. It was a big game for many of the players. At the end of the day the final was a good game and we played well against a good team.'

Did this mean he had edged out Ruud as first-choice striker?

'No. For me I didn't see it that way. Maybe people outside the club did, but it's the rotation system and sometimes you play well and sometimes you don't. Sometimes you play well but you don't win, so it's about getting results. I wasn't happy to be in the team like that, but just to be here and to do our best and that's what we are doing.

'Of course it was good to score and to get the trophy so it was the perfect day, but it's not easy to repeat that every time. Every game is different and every opponent is different, so you have to keep working hard to make sure you are not surprised if you don't succeed.'

Was there sympathy for Ruud?

'I think that's the life of a striker. It's very difficult to keep your place every time and there are so many games around so you can have peak form or sometimes drop form and it's always the same. You can see many big clubs do that, but I just concentrate on my game. The team spirit and teamwork is my main concern really. It's nice to win something and I was proud for sure, and the League Cup was a way to win a trophy this time, so I will take it.

'I would say there was something more special than winning the cup; it was about getting more confidence. It was my first trophy so that was very important, to think you can win things. You haven't run over a black cat or something like that, so it was very good. It was a first for Wayne as well, and things like that are very important.'

Sir Alex explained the thinking behind United's apparent laid-back approach.

'The romance was always there with Wigan and that is why we didn't go over the top. We got criticism for not having special press days and all the rest of it, but if we had done that we wouldn't have got any coverage anyway. We aren't stupid. They must think we are all daft here.

'It was Wigan's day, so let them go and enjoy it and quite rightly. Let all the publicity go to them, plus the fact that I wanted to know something about their players that perhaps I didn't already know. I was reading stuff about Wigan players that I wasn't aware of.

'They had their press day on Monday and I was able to spend the week picking up things about their players from the interviews they gave. You have to make sure you take care of all the little details and some of the things you didn't know about them could be important!'

With Wembley Stadium likely to be reopened in 2007, the final seemed likely to be United's last appearance in Cardiff and that was something which meant more to a reflective Ryan Giggs than any of his team-mates.

'It's my home town and all my family were there to see the game and it's been great playing in finals there. Wembley is special, but for me to go to the Millennium and to win something. That has been special to me. 'We've won a couple of cups there now, but I have also lost a couple so there are mixed fortunes, but it was great winning something in Cardiff again.

'Even though they say the Carling Cup is down in our priorities, there's still the build-up and going there and seeing the fans coming down to the stadium. Everything surrounding a cup final is something special.

'The build-up to a final is different. You get up for breakfast preparing yourself for the game, later in the morning we have the team talk, then something light to eat. Then comes the coach journey to the stadium. On the way you see the United fans, the Wigan fans, and that's when you start to get excited.

'You see the stadium and when you get there there's even more fans. It's tremendous and playing under the closed roof always reminds me of a night game even though it's the middle of the afternoon. I know I play there for Wales, but it is always that bit more special when you go with your club.'

Could Carling Cup success act as a springboard to greater things? It had done in the past.

'It was the first trophy that I ever won and it gives you a taste of success. It lets you know what United is all about: winning trophies, doing the lap of honour, having a medal. This is the first trophy for many of the players, so hopefully it can do what it did for me and give them that taste for success that makes you want more. That's what I hope it does to the players who have come into the team recently.'

Rio Ferdinand was not a recent acquisition, but he was one of those to enjoy the new experience.

'It's the first cup competition I have won after being in a couple of finals and being on the losing side. It's just a great feeling and people might harp on about it only being the League Cup, but for me a cup competition is a cup competition. You don't go in it to lose, you go in it to win it and we managed to do that.

'It was a great day, but we were lucky in a sense that we went a few goals up before the end of the game and you could kind of relax a little bit and take it all in. It was one of those games where we were on a hiding to nothing because everybody expected us to go out and win, so we had to put a performance in and we actually did that.

'Wigan were fairly good, but I think we just outplayed them all over the park and managed to get the result we wanted. The midfield and forwards played magnificently and we created enough chances to have been three up in the first half. In the second half, we came out and just finished the game off.'

Was there a moment that stood out for him?

'Wazza's second goal, our fourth. I just knocked it down to him and he scored and that just said to me: "The game's over, we've won. We can't lose now." It's great when you get that feeling during a game. You can then enjoy the occasion.

'In most big pressure games, I suppose that applies to most games, you don't get time to enjoy it perhaps, until you maybe look back on your career and think, "Yeah, I played there and I enjoyed that." But you finish a game and maybe have that night to think about it, then next day you are on to another. You don't really get time to dwell. Probably if you do your season can come to a halt.

'Going up and getting the medal was a good moment too, looking at it and seeing it said "winners" rather than "runners up". That was great. I have two runners-up medals and they are kind of disappointing to have in your possession, but a winners' medal is a great feeling and a great achievement. It's going in a cupboard at home and hopefully I will be able to add a few more before I start getting them out to go on show.'

And what of 'Wazza' Rooney? Back at Carrington he relived the day.

'It was brilliant. Exciting. The build-up to the game was great. I had played in the FA Cup final last year, so it was similar in a way, but after losing like we did, we knew we had to win this game. A lot of effort and desire went into winning that trophy and into the way we played and we fully deserved the win. Believe me, winning any trophy is brilliant.'

But no night on the town after the game?

'No. The journey home was good. We flew back so it was a fairly short trip, but we couldn't really celebrate too much because we were off to international games, so that was a bit of a downer, but these things happen. We had to keep our minds right for the games for our country through the week.'

John O'Shea's recollection of the afternoon was one of immense satisfaction.

'It couldn't have gone any better for us. To win 4–0 when we had everything to lose. There was a lot of pressure on us, but we gave a great account of ourselves. I've had my share of honours and this one was just as big a buzz as the others. It was a first for Wayne, and for Vida and Patrice Evra, who had just come to the club, their first experience of the success and the feeling it gives you and makes you want more.'

He also revealed that he had tried some good-natured skulduggery before the game by telling one or two white lies to Republic of Ireland team-mate Graham Kavanagh, the Wigan midfielder.

'Kav and I exchanged a few texts. I kept telling him, "I'm not going to be fit, I'm not going to be playing." But I knew I would be! We spoke a little bit during the game, although you never really remember what you have been saying, but he has done great there this season and the experience he has given Wigan for their first season in the Premiership was vital.'

Did any memory of the final stand out?

'It's always hard to pick out moments, especially from a game like that. We had a couple of early chances, one from Wayne in particular and Louis, too. We also had a penalty claim turned down and you start thinking when they didn't go our way, "Crikey it's not going to be." Wigan also had a decent chance that Edwin saved, but the next thing I knew Wayne was put through again and he made sure this time. That really settled us down when he scored, and we just went on from there.

'I don't remember much about the celebrations afterwards. They go so quickly and you have to have a look at the DVD to see what actually happened, but you will always remember it because, no matter what people say, when you play in a final, be it the FA Cup, the Carling Cup or the European Cup, it could be your last final because of the sort of things that can happen in football. You have to make sure if you are picked, that you do enjoy it and the best way to do that is by winning.'

And if you are not in the side? Darren Fletcher's day was different.

'It's actually harder watching from the sidelines because you are biting your nails all the time. You would rather be out there playing, but you do your best to get behind the team and make sure you shake everyone's hand, wish them all the best and gee them up a little bit for the game.

'We had been down in the hotel for a couple of days preparing for the game so all the team were together. We actually trained in Swansea and the whole occasion was brilliant. We put on our cup final suits and got ourselves ready in the morning and it really is a special atmosphere when you walk out on the pitch and soak things in. It's a cup final. It doesn't matter whether it is the Carling Cup, the FA Cup or whatever, it's an important final and a trophy.

'The day's magnificent: your family are there, everyone's family and friends are there, and after the game when you are celebrating, it's a really special moment. Celebrating afterwards in the dressing room as a team and to have achieved something is great.

'I have started the two FA Cup finals and was left out this year, but on the whole it was great for the club to win and my personal disappointments aside you have to experience them in football.'

What was it like watching from the wings?

'We were huge favourites, even though Wigan did well to get to the final, and being the first trophy of the season we wanted to win it. In the end we won a trophy and maybe that is the first silverware for this team and we can push on and definitely challenge for the Premiership next season, and bigger and better things like Europe.'

Little was made of Fletcher's absence, but the same could not be said about the exclusion of van Nistelrooy. The Dutchman's name was in the headlines for the rest of the week amid claims that Sunday's move marked the beginning of the end for the striker.

Sir Alex clarified the situation.

'There was a danger of losing Louis if I hadn't played him in the final after he had scored so many goals. He might say: "I can get a regular place somewhere else," and Louis would have been disappointed if he hadn't played. He scored goals throughout the competition, including in both legs of the semi-final, which is some feat. He deserved to play in the final and everything else is secondary.'

It was not the first time the manager had made a key decision in a final.

For the 1990 FA Cup replay against Crystal Palace, goalkeeper Jim Leighton was dropped with Les Sealey coming into the side and remaining there as first choice the following season. After leaving Bryan Robson out of the Double-completing final of 1994, Sir Alex followed an identical route two years later, this time another captain Steve Bruce, came to the end of his days at Old Trafford and was omitted from the side that won the FA Cup to secure the 'double Double'.

'Go back to a few years ago when we had the four strikers, Andy Cole, Dwight Yorke, Teddy Sheringham and Ole Gunnar Solskjaer. It was always difficult when we picked teams then.

'There was always disappointment. Everybody wants to play in a game of football, particularly a final. Young Darren was left out completely and he's been involved almost all season. He's had to cope with playing with different midfield players but he's always been available. He's probably played with six or seven different players alongside him this year – Roy Keane, Paul Scholes, John O'Shea, Kieran Richardson, Ryan Giggs, Alan Smith – but the boy kept on going.

'The boy would be disappointed not to play in the final so it's always difficult, but players benefit from competition, whether it's from their own team-mates or the opponents they are playing against. At this moment in time, the team has got competition because it has a challenge on its hands to be second in the league.'

This was a new tack from the manager. The Carling Cup was over. He had to concentrate on the next Premiership outing, which just happened to be against Wigan at the JJB, but it did seem as though he was ready to concede the title race.

CHAPTER EIGHT

King Louis reigns but the title dream fades

The suggestion that Sir Alex might be getting ready to throw in the towel raised many an eyebrow. Giving up was totally out of character for a man who, in past years, had seen his side overhaul runaways Newcastle and Arsenal to snatch Premiership crowns and come back from the dead when the Champions League seemed lost, to secure his greatest honour in 1999.

'It's never over till it's over,' was always the Ferguson view, yet here he was admitting that second best would be good enough for Manchester United and for that reason his comments were viewed with cynicism in some quarters. The old fox was playing mind games again, according to some sections of the media. Was it an attempt to coax Mourinho into taking his foot off the gas or to bluff Chelsea's players into relaxed mode, thinking that the race was over? We would see.

As March began, there was a mathematical possibility of catching Chelsea, but it would need the Londoners to slip seriously, and that had not been part of their make-up for two seasons. They were, after all, a comfortable eighteen points ahead of the Reds as Sir Alex prepared for the short trip to Wigan's JJB Stadium.

What was more important, considering the manager's declaration, was that their involvement in the cup final had meant they had played two games fewer than both Chelsea and Liverpool, with the Merseysiders stepping over them into second place.

There was a plus side though. While Chelsea won at West Brom two days before United's game at Wigan, Liverpool were held to a goalless draw at home by Charlton. Provided they could win, when it came to regaining second spot, the scales had tipped slightly in United's favour.

'We are taking it that Chelsea are not going to throw the league away, but it's important for us to be second,' the manager professed. 'The challenge is always to be there. You get challenges in different directions and football is full of that. I am sure the players realise how important it is to be second, so hopefully we can be consistent right until the end of the season and get that second spot.'

On the eve of the final, Sir Alex had watched the Portsmouth–Chelsea game on television at the team hotel, hoping deep down that Harry Redknapp's side would pull off a major shock. It was not to be.

'I don't think anyone is expecting Chelsea to throw the league away, but there were long periods where you thought Portsmouth might be going to get something out of the game because they were fighting against relegation, but Lampard scored. Again. That changed the whole picture.'

Could United change the picture before the finishing line?

'We'll see. But we have a challenge again tonight. Having won against Wigan a week ago you know it is going to be even more difficult going to their ground. It's going to be an open game and that's where Wigan get such great credit this year. They have got their results by having a go and they have had some fantastic results through that. They have good attacking players.

'They had a lot of opportunities on Sunday and we did well blocking shots. While they had their opportunities, we took ours. Those three quick goals in the second half were a killer for them and they probably didn't deserve it. Their attitude to the game was good, the spirit it was played in between the two sets of players meant there was never a problem in the match. 'Wigan are an attacking side and so are we. It should be a good game.'

It was.

MONDAY 6 MARCH 2006

SCORER:
Ronaldo 74,
own goal 90

ATTENDANCE:
22,524

Barclays Premiership
Wigan Athletic 1   Manchester United 2

UNITED: VAN DER SAR, NEVILLE, FERDINAND, BROWN, SILVESTRE (EVRA 85), RONALDO, O'SHEA, GIGGS, PARK (VAN NISTELROOY 71), ROONEY, SAHA. SUBS NOT USED: HOWARD, VIDIC, RICHARDSON.

Surprise one: Ruud van Nistelrooy was in the squad, despite Sir Alex virtually ruling him out after he had withdrawn from Holland's midweek international suffering from a stomach bug. Again Louis Saha started, with Ruud on the bench, but this time he was called upon.

Surprise two: Wigan pushed United all the way, scored first and, after a spirited performance, deserved to take something from a thrilling game.

Sir Alex named the squad he had used in the cup final, while Wigan were without unlucky 'keeper Mike Pollitt, so John Filan was again in goal with another United old boy Gary Walsh, Wigan's goal-keeping coach, on the bench. Unlike Pollitt, Walsh had played first team football during his days at Old Trafford and was Peter Schmeichel's deputy for part of the first Premiership-winning season in 1992–93.

It was United's first competitive outing at the small, but perfect-ly formed, JJB where they had appeared in 1999 as the new stadium opened, on a night when Paul Scholes and Ole Gunnar Solskjaer scored, but neither were in the squad for this one as Wigan went at United from the start.

Gary Teale twice went close, Jason Roberts tested Edwin van der Sar then the Rooney–Ronaldo–Saha combination clicked at the other end, with the French striker almost scoring. Henri Camara shot wide in the thirty-fifth minute, Graham Kavanagh's 25-yard effort dipped over the bar, then right on half time, Roberts was only inch-es away with a powerful drive. It was so different from Cardiff, espe-cially when Paul Scharner scored after de Zeeuw and Roberts had seen Ryan Giggs block their chances on the line.

On came Ruud in the seventy-first minute and, within ninety seconds, he had played a part in United's equaliser. Ronaldo sent him away on the right. Ruud broke forward and returned the gesture for the waiting Ronaldo to tuck home.

Who said anything about giving up?

Two minutes' stoppage time had been played when United broke. Ronaldo sprinted upfield and hammered the ball into Wigan box. Saha struck, his fierce shot pounded against the underside of the bar, forcing Pascal Chimbonda to make a desperate clearing lunge that sent the ball into his own net. So cruel on Wigan, but it was a win that put United back into second place.

'That was a fantastic game. Breathtaking stuff and Wigan were terrific in the first half,' was the manager's after-whistle reaction. 'They gave us a right doing and I thought we were lucky to go in 0–0 at half time. We had to get them in, get things sorted out and get on with our game in a proper way, but they just kept coming at us and deserved to be in front.

'In fairness to our players, we did start to play after we lost the goal and there was far more impetus and more energy about our game and we maybe deserved the equaliser. I don't think we deserved to win. Wigan have been very unlucky. That's the hardest game we have had away from home this season, yet we have managed to get a result out of it.

'This was a big opportunity for us tonight and we have taken it. Maybe we didn't deserve it, but we have taken it and it's a reminder that we never give in. That is the one quality that Manchester United have: they just don't stop.'

Sir Alex had again left Ruud van Nistelrooy out his starting line-up. How difficult a task had that been?

'It just goes back to the team winning last Sunday. If he had been playing in the cup final and had scored a goal in a 4–0 victory you would expect him to play in the next game. That's what it was about. That's the name of the game. I am delighted I have got competition from my strikers and I've got little Rossi, and Ole Gunnar coming back. It's good.'

Wes Brown felt the win was as crucial as victory in Cardiff.

'It was very important. We are driving for that second place and this was a tough game for us, but we have come through with a late win, which is great. At times they were the better team, especially in the first half, and they scored a good goal. But we didn't stop and it paid off.

'Rio and I had our hands full all night with Roberts and Camara. They are two very strong, fast players and they made it very hard and that's what you come up against in the Premiership. We knew they were going to give us trouble, but we handled them well.

'When they scored, I don't think we panicked. We kept going and, if anything, it lifted us that little bit and after we got the first goal it was a case of whether we could go on and nick it, and we did. It was unlucky for them, but it was a tough game for us and we knew how important it was. If we had slipped up tonight it would have let Liverpool in, but now it gives us that little gap and we will just have to keep going onto the next game. We've got eleven games to go, seven of them at home and that's good.'

For Gary Neville, a ninety-second-minute winner was nothing new.

'It's something we have become renowned for over the years and it's great when you do it because there's no comeback for the other team. That's the best time to win a game, although we prefer to be three– or four–nil up!

'Tonight it took them to go in front to make us start playing. We never really got going in the first half and they put us under a lot of pressure. We knew this would be more difficult than the other two games we've played against them this season, you just knew. The atmosphere of them playing in front of their own fans, the fact that we had beaten them last week and earlier in the season in quite a convincing manner. It was never going to be the same and they certainly put us under a lot of pressure and probably deserved more.

'If I was a neutral I would feel sorry for Wigan. I don't want to patronise them, but for the overall performance and effort they put in, they should have got something. But we kept going and you have to give us some credit.'

What were the captain's thoughts when the three-minute board went up at the end?

'You are playing for United and you know three minutes is a long time. We have won big tournaments in three minutes, so we know we can score one goal. We have scored so many late goals over the years that three minutes isn't a problem, you just have to think, "Keep going, keep passing the ball in the right way and hopefully something will come." We always ask for one chance. We got one and thankfully it went in, and that keeps us on track for where we want to be.

'We faltered badly last season when we knew we couldn't catch Chelsea. We are fifteen points behind them, we do have a game in hand, but there are so few games left it's going to be difficult for us to catch them, so we have to cement that second place. It's important we don't have to go and play a European qualifier; we have talked about it and it ruins your whole pre-season, your build-up in terms of when players come back as well as the difficulty of having to qualify for the Champions League. It is not always cut and dried, so we want to make sure we do our job to the end of the season. We owe it to the fans to put in good performances and we are capable of doing that.'

What about that run-in of seven home games?

'Earlier in the season we struggled at Old Trafford, but in the last few months we have done quite well, although it seems ages since we played there. On Sunday we have a really good game to look forward to. Newcastle against Manchester United is always a great game, plenty of goals, usually great ones as well, so we hope we can keep the run going and the confidence from tonight will show through.'

It had been five weeks since United last played at home and while the majority of the media still appeared pre-occupied about Ruud van Nistelrooy's future, there was a major blow for another of Sir Alex's strike force during the build up to the Newcastle game.

After almost two years out, Ole Gunnar Solskjaer, so close to re-establishing himself in the first team, had fractured a cheekbone playing in a reserve game against Middlesbrough, the night after the Wigan win.

Sir Alex sympathised: 'I watched the game and it was a really clumsy challenge by Ugo Ehiogu. He really clattered into Ole. It was an accident, but for Ole to get that after coming back and doing so well was a killer blow. But we are already looking to the future for Ole and we will see what we can do.'

And Alan Smith?

'He is making good progress; we are hoping to get the plaster off in the next ten days, then he will go into a supportive boot and we will be able to start his rehabilitation in the gymnasium, so hopefully it's all systems go.'

The talk about strikers deflected attention away from an area of the team that had suddenly started to look more settled. The return of John O'Shea from his rib injury, plus the recovery of Ryan Giggs from the hamstring problem that caused him to miss the last home game, meant that Old Trafford would see the dynamic duo for the first time.

Ryan was enjoying his new role as a central midfielder and was looking forward to the challenge Newcastle would provide.

'We are two teams who like to score goals, like to play football and usually there are goals whether it's at Old Trafford or at St James'. We hope we can carry on our record against them, but they are doing great at the moment,' he said.

Newcastle were indeed coming to Old Trafford on the back of their best run of the season. It had started after manager Graeme Souness was sacked on 1 February, following a 3–0 defeat against Manchester City.

Former West Ham manager Glenn Roeder was brought in from the club's coaching ranks and given temporary charge, a move which appeared to have injected new enthusiasm into the ranks. The

Magpies were on a six-game unbeaten run in all competitions, with four wins and a draw in their last five Premiership outings.

'That happens so often when clubs change managers. The team starts getting results, so they'll be confident going into this one thinking they can get a result. I don't know why that happens, maybe it's because players who weren't in the side start getting in and think they have a point to prove to whoever comes in. I don't know what it is, but it always seems to happen,' Ryan added.

The magic had to wear off some time.

SUNDAY 12 MARCH 2006

Barclays Premiership
Manchester United 2   Newcastle United 0

SCORER:
Rooney 8, 12

ATTENDANCE:
67,858

UNITED: VAN DER SAR, NEVILLE, FERDINAND, BROWN, SILVESTRE (EVRA 46), RONALDO (VAN NISTELROOY 75), O'SHEA, GIGGS, PARK, ROONEY, SAHA. SUBS NOT USED: HOWARD, VIDIC, ROSSI

Alan who? As the veteran Shearer made his last appearance against United, the club whose advances he rejected twice, turning down moves to Old Trafford when with Southampton and later Blackburn Rovers, it was fitting that the player who has inherited his mantle as England's main man should run the show, quite literally.

Wayne Rooney was in breathtaking form. With boundless energy, he pounded the Old Trafford turf, ploughing a permanent furrow towards the Newcastle penalty area and how he was restricted to just two goals was down to some splendid keeping by Ireland international Shay Given, by some bad luck and by a little bit of indifferent finishing.

Rooney's first came after only eight minutes and Newcastle right-back Craig Ramage had to take most of the blame. He tried to pick out Given with a back pass, but Rooney pounced and dinked the ball beautifully over the 'keeper to the delight of the home fans.

Four minutes later, the twenty-year-old did it again, this time from John O'Shea's pass, with Rooney running forward and poking his shot beyond the 'keeper to make everyone think a rout was on the cards.

It never happened. Two goals in twelve minutes, none in the remainder of a one-sided game that saw Ruud van Nistelrooy come off the bench for his 211th appearance, but the game ended with him still two goals away from 150.

Sir Alex was openly delighted by what he had seen: 'Wayne Rooney was absolutely marvellous. Apart from the chances created by his team-mates, I felt his own determination, tenacity and dribbling skills, which created opportunities for himself, were absolutely marvellous to watch. For the first goal he had the imagination, the courage and the daring to chip the goalkeeper, which he did.

'We had twenty-nine goal-scoring opportunities this afternoon and that must come close to the best we have played at home this season. Right from the word go, our penetration and passing in the front part of the pitch was very good. I was really pleased, but it got to a point where I was starting to laugh to myself because of the number of missed chances. It almost became a comedy, but you know in football, if you don't get that third chance to put yourself in the safety zone then you can lose a goal that changes the whole picture. Fortunately our defending was excellent and we never looked like losing a goal, but you are still on tenterhooks until you reach that safety margin.'

And the Saha–Rooney partnership, which had again begun the game?

'They are doing fine. They are very good together. Louis's form has been great. He has shown great tenacity. He's quick, he's aggressive, he's good in the air, two great feet. I think we are looking at an outstanding centre-forward and we are fortunate with Wayne and Ruud, and young Rossi coming through, that we are getting to the competition we wanted and have been looking for, for quite a while.'

Could United better that target of second place?

'I can only look at our own form. I think we should just go and enjoy our football, take each game as it comes along and try and win the matches, and see where it goes.'

Hopes of taking that runner-up spot received a major boost three hours after the Newcastle win as Liverpool ended a dismal week by losing 2–1 Highbury. Four days earlier they had gone out of the Champions League after losing 2–0 at home to Benfica, so it was advantage United as far as the contest for second place was concerned.

However, as United got ready for the trip to The Hawthorns, where West Bromwich Albion were fighting to survive in the Premiership, Liverpool bounced back, thrashing Fulham 5–1 at Anfield to tip the see-saw once again.

Another must-win Saturday was coming up, but forty-eight hours before the game, Sir Alex, the majority of the club's playing staff, plus most of the Old Trafford hierarchy, attended a memorial service for George Best in Manchester Cathedral.

Calum Best and George's team-mates from the sixties were also present for what the Dean of Manchester, the Very Reverend Roger Govender described as, 'Manchester's chance to say goodbye.'

The following day, the manager travelled to Glasgow for the funeral of former Scotland star Jimmy Johnstone. Among the other mourners was Roy Keane, there with his new team-mates from Johnstone's old club Celtic. Sir Alex and his former skipper met for the first time since their parting of the ways four months earlier.

'I spoke to him briefly and there are no hard feelings,' he revealed on his return.

It was obvious Keane had settled in well at Parkhead and, reflecting on events which had caused such a stir in November, Sir Alex added.

'It was just two adult people getting together and agreeing on what was the best thing for both parties. I think going to Celtic was a great thing for him, because at many points in his life he was always a Celtic fan. I read all this stuff about him always being a Celtic fan, but I reckon he was a Man United fan always, but he had a leaning towards Celtic, which is understandable with the Irish connection Celtic have. They are a big club. It is a terrific club Celtic Football Club.'

Coming from former Rangers striker Alex Ferguson, that is praise indeed!

In his absence, it was Carlos Queiroz who faced the media before the game at West Brom, and it was obvious that he had been well briefed about what to expect. He had hardly taken his seat when the questions about Ruud van Nistelrooy began.

'It's a big club Manchester United, with big stars and the speculation will always be around us and I don't see anything wrong with that. It's part of the game, part of the show and as long as it doesn't cross the limits there is no problem about that. The most important thing in my view is that Ruud is a crucial player for our goals and our ambitions. Nobody can have any doubts about that. He is part of our family, part of our team, part of our needs. His contribution, starting a game or coming on during a game, is always crucial for us.'

He continued, commenting on the squad rotation system United have used so often over the years: 'We have twenty-three players and there was one part of the season when Cristiano didn't play a couple of games, Ji-Park didn't play, Wayne was out. There is nothing wrong with that.'

'What is important is the outcome of the team. We are doing well, we are performing well, scoring goals. The contribution of the players is there. No complaints, let's move forward because we have thirty points in front of us for the rest of the season.'

The first of those were up for grabs at The Hawthorns.

'It's a must-win situation for West Brom and for us it's also very important because we can't afford to lose one point. It is a team that needs to win against a team that wants to win. It'll be difficult, it'll be tough, but I believe we can do it.'

He also took a different view from the manager.

'Our goal, our race is not to finish second. I don't want to put things that way. We have enough points at the moment and enough in front of us to have more. Chelsea are five or six wins from the trophy, let's see if they can do it because they also have to face teams who are in that must-win situation. Our goal is only the points, to win game after game and if Chelsea keep this situation then our goal will be second position. Let's see what happens.'

SATURDAY 18 MARCH 2006

Barclays Premiership
West Bromwich Albion 1   Manchester United 2

UNITED: VAN DER SAR, NEVILLE, FERDINAND, VIDIC, SILVESTRE, RONALDO, O'SHEA, GIGGS, RICHARDSON (FLETCHER 89), ROONEY, SAHA. SUBS NOT USED: HOWARD, EVRA, VAN NISTELROOY, ROSSI.

SCORER:
Saha 16, 64
ATTENDANCE:
27,623

Louis Saha again paid back the faith being shown in him by Sir Alex as he kept his starting place. With Ruud van Nistelrooy on the bench, the French star's goals carried United to another victory, making it five in a row since that last Premiership defeat at Blackburn.

A goal in each half was enough to see United through and even though Albion staged a late fightback, the Reds rarely appeared troubled. United went ahead after sixteen minutes when Saha rose to head home a Ryan Giggs corner with the Albion defence nowhere to be seen. His second came almost an hour later, with Cristiano Ronaldo doing the running and laying on the final ball. There was a scare when Nathan Ellington scored from Jonathan Greening's corner to give Albion hope, but from then on United stood firm.

For one member of the United side, the trip to The Hawthorns was a return to familiar surroundings, somewhere that has a place in Kieran Richardson's heart. A year earlier, he had temporarily worn the blue and white of Albion during a loan spell that proved a major career boost for the twenty-one-year old from Greenwich.

Regular first-team football, as The Baggies survived in the Premiership, earned him a call-up for England's summer tour to America and, after turning down the chance to make the move to the Midlands permanent, he was back at Old Trafford and a regular in the senior squad.

'I remember being on the motorway when I got the call from

Ricky Sbragia, the United reserve team coach, telling me that Bryan Robson wanted me at West Brom. He just said, "Ring him. Here's his number." It was great. Bryan is a legend and I thought it would be a good move for me because it would be good to work under him. I suppose I was a bit shy at first, but once I settled in I was right in there enjoying it. It was a great learning curve and I came back a better player. I had a great time there.'

The midfielder has adjusted to his new role as a left-back: 'It's a bit harder to score goals, but I am sure I will get some before the end of the season. The main thing for me is that I'm playing and I don't care what position I play in.'

The win kept United two points ahead of Liverpool, but the following day the balloon went up when Chelsea lost 1–0 to neighbours Fulham at Craven Cottage. The gap was down to twelve points, United had a game in hand and they still had to go to Stamford Bridge. Surely not? But John O'Shea was keeping his fingers crossed.

'There's a slight, slight hope, and you have to think like that because you never know. They have been going through a rocky patch, but when you see the players that they have, you know they can get the results when they need them, so we'll have to wait and see. We are just focusing on one game at a time and we have some hard games coming up. We have to play teams fighting against relegation, some fighting for European places, Champions League places, so there is still plenty to play for yet.'

In the week between the West Brom win and Birmingham's visit to Old Trafford, Sir Alex and several of the first team players joined Sir Bobby Charlton for a unique event at the club's Academy complex to commemorate the legendary Busby Babes.

With 2006 marking the 50th anniversary of the first league title win by the side torn apart by the Munich Air Disaster, the club launched a new charity – the Manchester United Foundation – to benefit young people locally and worldwide.

Not surprisingly the emphasis was on youth as Cristiano Ronaldo, Giuseppe Rossi and Gerard Pique were joined by Rio Ferdinand, Ryan Giggs, Wes Brown and Edwin van der Sar, for a special training session involving eighty youngsters from local schools, with Sir Alex looking back on what was a memorable era for the club: 'That period was an incredible one in United's history, but the real story started after Munich in '58 when Sir Matt Busby rebuilt the club and led them to the European Cup ten years later. People were captivated by the courage of United and its manager, as well as the number of young players that he brought through into the team; that's never left us.

'When I first came to the club one of my main aims was to reinvigorate our youth system to the level that we've now reached, but I'm always looking ahead and trying to improve things. What we do well at this club is develop young players to a level that will take them far in the game.'

Four of the players involved in the event – Giggs, Ferdinand, van der Sar and Ronaldo – were on duty again four days later as another of the clubs battling to stay in the Premiership stood between United and three points, as Steve Bruce brought Birmingham City to Old Trafford. The return to his former club could not have come at a worse time.

In midweek, Birmingham had been knocked out of the FA Cup, beaten 7–0 at home by Liverpool, a result Carlos Queiroz sportingly tried to play down: 'Our view is that terrible defeat never happened. We have to ignore that result. Those kind of results belong to the fantasy world. All we know on Sunday is, it is a team, players, Steve, a club fighting for survival and it won't be easy for us.'

It was also an important day for Gary Neville: his 500th appearance for United would be a feat achieved by only seven others before him. The new captain found himself alongside Sir Bobby Charlton, Bill Foulkes, Alex Stepney, Tony Dunne, Joe Spence and Denis Irwin, as well as Ryan Giggs, in an elite band, but in typical fashion was already looking ahead to the next 500!

'I hope to be able to play for the club for as long as possible. It isn't measured by the amount of appearances, it's just measured season to season and hopefully I can still be in the squad at the start of the new season. I am desperate to play for this club, desperate as ever to win trophies. I love playing for United. United has given me everything and I am not stupid enough to think there is something better for me elsewhere.'

And being captain?

'With Roy leaving there was a vacancy in the captaincy and the manager gave it to me. I was delighted to take it. Over the years, the players I have respected most at this club have been the captains: Bryan Robson, Steve Bruce, Eric Cantona, Roy Keane.

'I have enjoyed the captaincy and also the form we have shown in the last three months. It has been fantastic. I have also enjoyed playing in what is a young team, one that is getting better and better and has certainly improved over that time. Winning the Carling Cup has given us a level of confidence and we seem to have gone on from that. Having the captaincy was the biggest honour I could have as a football player, growing up as a United fan. All my heroes have been the captains of United.'

And which one of them is in you? A bit of all of them?

'No, not really. They were what you would call great players and I don't think I have the same level as them, but there are other qualities that I believe I have that people can look up to in different ways and I just hope that I can lift trophies for the club and that the team can become successful.'

Fellow 500-club member Giggs gave an insight into life under captain Neville.

'Gazza has always been vocal. Everyone knows that and I think he is enjoying being captain. He is a fan through and through and to become captain is brilliant for him. He deserves it, but he hasn't changed that much. He has always been vocal, ever since he came into the team, and he has always been an organiser both on and off the pitch. He is the one who organises team days out or whatever, so not a lot has changed really.

Has he got better or worse?

'That's impossible! For Nev to get worse or get louder or more vocal, that's impossible. But he has done a brilliant job and he has won a trophy as well, so that was great for him.'

SUNDAY 26 MARCH 2006

Barclays Premiership
Manchester United 3   Birmingham City 0

UNITED: VAN DER SAR, NEVILLE, FERDINAND, VIDIC, SILVESTRE, RONALDO, O'SHEA, GIGGS (FLETCHER 77), RICHARDSON (PARK 39), ROONEY, SAHA (VAN NISTELROOY 73). SUBS NOT USED: HOWARD, EVRA.

SCORERS:
Own goal 3,
Giggs 15,
Rooney 83

ATTENDANCE:
69,070

Fitting perhaps that the hero of this one should be Ryan Giggs, chalking up his 664th appearance, as United hit Birmingham's hopes of survival from as early as the third minute. Ryan's ferocious free kick gave Maik Taylor no chance, but the unfortunate 'keeper hardly wanted to be credited with an own goal into the bargain. The Giggs rocket slammed against the Brum bar and bounced into the net off the back of the unfortunate Taylor's head as he flew across goal, but there was no argument about goal number two.

This came after fifteen minutes, when Giggs and Wayne Rooney worked a one-two and Ryan finished with a left-foot shot inside the far post. After that 7–0 hammering in midweek, United fans were wondering if there might be a repeat, but it was not until the eighty-third minute that goal three came, with a running Rooney picking up a headed pass from Ronaldo before hitting a powerful shot beyond Taylor.

The game was watched by a crowd of 69,070; United's biggest for eighty-five years and all due to extension work being carried out at Old Trafford. With more seats being added every day, things could only get bigger.

A satisfying win for skipper Neville, but were the fans expecting a big score on the back of Birmingham's midweek debacle?

'Possibly, and we had to guard against complacency and make sure we tried to take as many of the chances we knew we would get at Old Trafford. We should have been three or four up at half time, but in the second half they did quite well and could've had a couple of goals. In the end we deserved the victory for our first-half performance.

'I can imagine what they were thinking after the other night when they conceded so early and it was a great free kick. They couldn't do too much about it. It was an unbelievable shot and they may think they were a bit unfortunate. The second was a great goal and that killed them. When you are down there I suppose it must be difficult, but we can't really afford to think about that. We've just got to do our job and make sure we get that second place and hopefully close in on Chelsea as near as we can.

'It was a good day for me, obviously, because we won. I'm happy to have played for this club for so long ... but I'm still a long way off Giggsy.'

For Barclays Man of the Match Ryan, the most important thing was the win, which took the Reds back above Liverpool, who had beaten Everton at Anfield the previous day.

'We have said we want to cement second place as soon as we can and these are the games we should be winning and thankfully we have, so we have to carry on the good form we have been showing. As long as the team's winning it doesn't matter who scores, that's Man United there are goal scorers all over the pitch and it's shown today, I got two, Wayne got one, but our form's been good and we just had to carry that on. Forget where Chelsea are in the table and just concentrate on our own form.'

It was the start of a big week.

There was little time for rest, with West Ham coming to Old Trafford three days after the Birmingham game then, three days later, the trip to Bolton.

'The form's been excellent over the last few weeks and I don't think we should be changing it,' was the most significant comment from Sir Alex after the game. Would Ruud van Nistelrooy again be out of the starting line-up?

Two days later, things had changed. Saha had picked up an injury during the Birmingham game and was doubtful, as the manager looked at the prospect of opening a five-point gap between second and third places.

'A gap like that might not be decisive at this stage, but it would be important. We've got to go to Chelsea, Bolton and Tottenham, three massive games away from home, but the way we are playing I don't think it matters who we play, but it's like everything else: you hope you don't get any serious injuries to your main players.'

WEDNESDAY 29 MARCH 2006

Barclays Premiership
Manchester United 1   West Ham United 0

UNITED: VAN DER SAR, PIQUE, FERDINAND, VIDIC, EVRA (SILVESTRE 78), RONALDO (SAHA 87), O'SHEA, FLETCHER (GIGGS 69), PARK, ROONEY, VAN NISTELROOY. SUBS NOT USED: HOWARD, ROSSI.

SCORER:
Van Nistelrooy 45
ATTENDANCE:
69,522

Ruud is back! The Dutchman started his first game since 18 February, and marked his return with the winning goal in front of another record crowd, this time of 69,522. Van the man got his 149th on the stroke of half time and, after having started the last five games on the bench, showed he had not lost his golden touch.

Others drafted in after the win over Birmingham were Gerard Pique, Patrice Evra, Darren Fletcher and Ji-sung Park, with Gary Neville ruled out because of a hamstring problem.

First-half stoppage time was underway as United broke the deadlock after some spirited threats from West Ham. Park made the goal with a brave run that took him past Paul Konchesky, before cutting the ball back for Ruud to side-foot home.

The second half saw Teddy Sheringham make a late appearance as West Ham tried to prise an equaliser out of a stubborn United defence and, as expected, the former Old Trafford star was given a great reception a week before his fortieth birthday. The gap to Chelsea was down to nine points.

'That was a typical Ruud goal,' said a satisfied Sir Alex. 'He is the best in Europe at that, without question, and what it does is gives us confidence in knowing we have three great strikers, and the potential of

Giuseppe Rossi also. When we were at our very best, with four great strikers, they won the European Cup, they won the Treble, they were one of the key factors that year and we can do that again if we can get four strikers competing for the position and we can rotate at the right moments. Louis Saha has been in great form, but we have a big game on Saturday and I have a difficult job picking my team now, but that's what I'm paid to do.'

Had van Nistelrooy done enough to edge out Saha?

That answer would come later in the week, but before then, the club announced that Ole Gunnar Solskjaer had signed a two-year contract extension, with more to the move than simply extending his playing career.

'His record here and the professionalism he has shown over the last decade and the goals he has scored, have made him an integral part of the success here,' said Sir Alex. 'He is a great role model for young people at this club, which we always need. We are encouraging him to take his coaching badges and I think this club needs role models in ambassadorial roles and we have to develop a bigger range of former players to fill them. This is a long-term view we are starting to consider.'

With the Bolton game twenty-four hours away, Sir Alex was finalising his plans and not for the first time, found himself faced with the problem of keeping all his strikers happy.

'It's exactly the same as when I had Teddy and Ole, and Andy and Dwight. When I was leaving two of them out they weren't happy, but they never threw their toys out of the pram. They stuck at it and we were winning things.

'The job was a lot easier when you had eleven players and a couple of subs. When I was at East Stirling, it was the easiest job in the world picking a team because you only had thirteen or fourteen players. We have twenty-three or twenty-four players, if you include the young ones, and what you have to do is try to be fair and let the player know the reasons why, which I always do.

'We're expecting a hard game, but it's not an issue. I enjoy the games with Bolton, but with the way we are playing we can accept any game at the moment. It's important for us to play the way we want to and handle the way Bolton play. Football is such an extra-ordinary game and full of surprises and that is why I have said all along that we want to be closest to Chelsea if they do collapse.'

So was that talk about finishing second a bluff after all?

SATURDAY 1 APRIL 2006

Barclays Premiership
Bolton Wanderers 1   Manchester United 2

UNITED: VAN DER SAR, NEVILLE, FERDINAND, VIDIC, SILVESTRE, RONALDO (PARK 89), FLETCHER (VAN NISTELROOY 60), O'SHEA, GIGGS, ROONEY, SAHA. SUBS NOT USED: HOWARD, EVRA, PIQUE.

SCORERS:
Saha 33,
Van Nistelrooy 79

ATTENDANCE:
27,778

Chelsea turned out to be the April Fools, dropping valuable points in a 0–0 draw at Birmingham City and turning this thrilling local derby into a game of even greater importance.

Sir Alex's big decision was made public shortly after 2 p.m. with Louis Saha getting the nod and Ruud van Nistelrooy on the bench; the manager got it spot on, because both scored.

The win came the hard way with Bolton, who had not lost at home since their opening game of the season, showing why they call their stadium Fortress Reebok as Kevin Davies gave them the lead after twenty-six minutes. Wanderers always threatened and when United did get through they found 'keeper Jussi Jaaskelainen on top form. It was their captain Kevin Nolan who created their goal, with a neat throughball to Davies who pushed it past Rio Ferdinand before firing home.

Bolton's delight lasted only seven minutes, as United's French connection struck. Mikael Silvestre broke down the left, threading the perfect pass to Saha, who hit a left-foot bender that no goalkeeper would have stopped. With half an hour left, Sir Alex withdrew Fletcher and sent on van Nistelrooy. The move paid off as he and Saha combined to set up the Dutchman for the winner and, after a long wait, his 150th goal for the club.

'That was a great result and the performance was one of determination and grit because the pitch wasn't very good. It was very difficult for both teams, so there wasn't any collective football, or not a lot of it anyway, and being 1–0 down under those circumstances you have to be concerned. But we showed our determination and got back to 1–1 and just kept on plugging away until we got the winner. Bolton improved in the second half and gave us some scary moments because they are such an organised and competent team and, at the end of it, I have to say that this is maybe our best result of the season,' was the Ferguson verdict.

He also gave the reason for Saha's recall.

'You have to assess these things. Ruud played his first game in five weeks on Wednesday and, three days later, going to Bolton is not the best preparation because it was quite a physical game against West Ham, not in terms of contact, but in terms of the running power of both teams. Ruud put a lot of energy into that game and I explained that to him and I think that he probably agreed with me for the first time.

'It's very difficult because great players want to play, but the important thing is we know that when he comes on we know what he is going to do, because he is the best finisher in the game. Next week he'll be fresh. Arsenal. A massive game now and it's a big consideration there.'

And Chelsea's slip at St Andrews?

'The Premiership race is still open simply because there are still games left to play. Our concentration is right on the game against Arsenal next Sunday; there will be close to 75,000 people at Old Trafford and we hope we can give them the performance to merit that attendance. We are playing well and, as Arsenal are playing well too, it should be a fantastic game.

'Then we have the situation where Chelsea have to come here to Bolton in two weeks' time and the pitch won't be as good as it was today because it will dry up by that time, then they have Blackburn away. Anything can happen. It's happened to us a few years ago when we lost the league to Arsenal the first time, but the important thing is that there's no use making silly predictions because seven points is a massive gap and it can still only be thrown away by Chelsea. It is getting closer. And we are playing well and that's the important issue.'

Wayne Rooney refused to look any higher than second place.

'We've been in great form and we've beaten some good sides. Personally, I've been happy with how it's going, so I just want to keep adding to the team and help us win games. The midfield has been doing really well recently. Giggsy and Sheasy have gone into the centre in the last few games and they've been solid and have been giving good service to the strikers. Fletch came back in again today and did a good job for us and we've got a few players coming back from injury now and the squad is getting bigger every week.

'We all know now we've got to play well to make sure we get in the team next time and it keeps us all on our toes. Hopefully that'll continue to keep the competition for places. The spirit is high, and we need to keep believing in ourselves. If we do that then we'll be there in the end, I think.'

Wayne also cast doubts about Chelsea's chances at The Reebok. 'It's a difficult place to go, especially with the pitch, which isn't the best around, as we saw. Their fans get right behind them as well, which also makes it difficult, but we did well under the circumstances and deserved the three points.'

With seven points separating the top two and Arsenal due at Old Trafford in three days, United's timing was impeccable as the club announced its biggest sponsorship deal in a tie-up with American insurance giants AIG. Chief executive David Gill saw it as a major step:

'It's a worldwide company, it's got a lot of assets we can use together; £56.5 million – it's great news for the club and all its fans around the world. It breaks down to just over £14 million a year; it's a record-breaking deal and it just shows that the strength of the club is still there and this is great for the future.'

AIG took over from Vodafone as United's shirt sponsors next season with Gill delighted to have not only found a replacement, but also to have vastly improved the cash injection the club receives from the move.

'We were clearly disappointed that Vodafone pulled out, but at the same time we expressed clear confidence that we would attract a great sponsor at new levels and that is an opinion that has now been vindicated. A lot of hard work has gone in by key people involved and to deliver the deal today is brilliant.'

This was the first major financial move of the new era at Old Trafford; the first to be completed since United had been bought by the Glazer family almost a year earlier.

Had the fact that the club was no longer a plc made things easier?

'Easier is probably not the right word, but it has certainly played a part. We are very experienced in football matters, but the new ideas and approach brought by the new directors has been very welcome and very useful. It's been very much a team effort to get to where we are today, to this fantastic position, and again it does vindicate the change in ownership.'

American owners, American sponsors ... did the two go together?

'That's very simplistic. We wanted to do what was the right deal for the club. AIG is one of the top five companies in the world; it is a huge organisation and we are buying into all of its strengths, all of its assets, around the world, not just the American angle.'

After the change of sponsor, a change of direction from Sir Alex.

Next day, as the build-up to the Arsenal game began, it was clear he was no longer prepared to live in Chelsea's shadow.

'It's a major opportunity for us. If we can win I think we have a very good chance of the league.

'I feel our form is very good and if your form is good in April then you have a chance. Given that we are seven points behind, the key is us winning and maintaining that form until we play Chelsea at Chelsea. We are in a closing position and, hopefully, if they do make another mistake and we can win our game on Sunday it might be a real test then. There's a lot of ifs about it.'

If ... United could beat Arsenal.

SUNDAY 9 APRIL 2006

Barclays Premiership
Manchester United 2   Arsenal 0

UNITED: VAN DER SAR, NEVILLE, FERDINAND, VIDIC, SILVESTRE, RONALDO, O'SHEA, GIGGS, PARK (EVRA 84), ROONEY, VAN NISTELROOY (SAHA 62). SUBS NOT USED: HOWARD, PIQUE, BROWN.

SCORERS:
Rooney 54,
Park 78

ATTENDANCE:
70,908

What a finish it could be. Earlier in the day, Chelsea showed their intent by hammering the Hammers 4–1, despite being reduced to ten men early in the game. Then this cracker, watched by 70,908, kept the status quo at the top. Yet for United to steal it, there had to be a Chelsea slip, but with games away to Bolton, Blackburn and Newcastle to complete their season and before that a home game against the Reds, there was clearly the possibility of that happening.

With van Nistelrooy starting and Saha on the bench, Rooney was in sensational form and chose the perfect day to do it as Old Trafford celebrated the fiftieth anniversary of the Busby Babes' first league title success in 1956.

The youthful Arsenal were no pushovers and caused a few scares in a first half that ended with justifiable penalty claims from the United camp and an almighty clanger from Graham Poll and his refereeing team.

A Ruud–Rooney move was completed when the England striker rounded Arsenal 'keeper Lehmann. He shot, but as the ball was heading goalwards Kolo Toure threw himself full length palming the shot onto a post. Handball? It was so blatant even Arsene Wenger must have seen it ... but not the officials. No penalty. No sending off and, at the break, no goals.

In the end justice was done in style. A run downfield by Silvestre, superb control from Rooney, who pulled the ball down on the run before hammering it home with barely a change of pace and, with fifty-four minutes gone, United were ahead.

Van Nistelrooy came off after an hour and on went Saha, with the

Frenchman's first scoring chance coming via a leaping header, but it was down to Ji-sung Park to tie things up. Rooney broke on the right, beat Senderos with strength and speed, crossed, and the little fellah from South Korea slid in to score a goal he will never forget.

'We had a go. We wanted to win the match and there was a great desire to do it,' said Sir Alex, who was still aggrieved about that penalty blunder. 'I have seen it on the television replay and it was definitely a penalty and that would have given them ten men, we would possibly have been 1–0 in the lead, but it didn't happen. We showed greater determination in the second half and I think we deserved to win.

'Wayne's goal was brilliant: that first touch. That was a glowing example to any footballer not only the first touch, but also to be able to set himself up for the shot at goal was outstanding. We could have scored more, but the most important thing for me today was the result and the performance.'

The gap between the Arsenal game and United's early start to the Easter programme was like the calm before the storm. The players went through their normal preparations, but with Sunderland due at Old Trafford on Good Friday evening, it meant a Maundy Thursday get together for media and manager.

'If we do our job, four points behind them, and they have to go to Bolton and we all know that is not the easiest place to go to. I am hopeful Bolton can do us a good turn and, if they do, if it's a draw or Bolton win, then it's a massive turnaround in the title race.'

It was also a massive turnaround for Sir Alex, who seemed to have settled for second spot not so long ago. As he had so often stressed, 'Easter can be the most important part of the season. We both have games on Monday. Our game at Tottenham is a major game for them, as well as us, because of Arsenal chasing them for fourth spot, so it's a really interesting league. But as I have said before, the league decider is at Stamford Bridge. If Chelsea win or draw that game then that's it over.'

There was a setback to his selection plans.

'Louis Saha got an injury in training yesterday. It's not serious and he may be on the bench tomorrow. He'll certainly be fit for Monday.'

Louis failed to make it. So did United.

FRIDAY 14 APRIL 2006

Barclays Premiership
Manchester United 0   Sunderland 0

ATTENDANCE:
72,519

UNITED: VAN DER SAR, NEVILLE, FERDINAND, BROWN, EVRA (SILVESTRE 68), RONALDO, O'SHEA (SOLSKJAER 68), GIGGS, PARK, ROONEY, VAN NISTELROOY. SUBS NOT USED: HOWARD, HEINZE, FORTUNE.

After nine league wins in a row, every United fan among the 72,519 inside Old Trafford came to the game convinced that number ten was on its way, with bottom club Sunderland providing the opposition. How wrong could they be? What was it Sir Alex had said two weeks earlier?

'Football is such an extraordinary game and full of surprises.'

Sunderland goalkeeper Kelvin Davis was one of them. He gave a performance that would not have looked out of place at the top of the table, making countless saves, making the manager's pre-game suggestion that this might be a chance to boost goal difference as little more than wishful thinking. Nothing would go right for Ronaldo and Rooney; Ruud could not crack a tight Black Cat defence; and United's best chances came from Ryan Giggs and Ji-sung Park, but they failed to score.

All eyes were now on Chelsea's trip to Bolton and, even though Sunderland took the first point away from Old Trafford in 2006, after the first Premiership 0–0 at home this season, it was not enough to keep them up.

Their supporters bemoaned relegation, but the disappointment was easily matched by that of United's following, who were stunned into silence after a frustrating night. Its one bright spot was the return of Ole Gunnar Solskjaer, who was brought on as a second-half substitute, but even the magical Norwegian could not conjure up anything to match that last-gasp winner of 1999.

'You have to say that's football,' gasped a shell-shocked Sir Alex as he reviewed events. 'You can never underrate the game and what it can do and that's why we have to cling to the hope that Bolton are going to beat Chelsea tomorrow. It may not happen, but you have to think that what happened here can happen somewhere else.

'It's not a question of it just being down to their goalkeeper, the whole team has worked its socks off. I thought they played very well, their best performance this season, but they could relax because they had nothing to protect or go for. They are relegated. In that sort of situation players can be uninhibited and enjoy themselves and they did that.

'The main factor of the night was our composure in the last third of the field. I have been saying all along that, with young players, you have to expect inconsistency. We know that Rooney and Ronaldo are going to be great players, without question. I would stake my life on that, but all the hype about placing that responsibility for England on Wayne Rooney has borne fruit tonight.

'People should remember he is only a kid and to say he is going to be responsible for England winning the World Cup is the biggest piece of nonsense I have ever heard in my life. Hopefully, what happened tonight tells everyone, this boy has got to learn. He's a kid, and Ronaldo has to learn also, but we know that. We are patient and we can wait two or three years to get the full potential from them. You fulfil potential not when they are twenty or twenty-one, but twenty-four or twenty-five. Tonight the two of them probably had their worst performances of the season, but we know they are great players.'

Was it time to wave the white flag?

'No. We have come too far. The form has been too good to give up. We have to dismiss tonight and say that if Sunderland can do it to us, then other teams can do it to Chelsea. I'm clinging to the hope that Bolton do us a favour tomorrow. Friends never let you down and

Sam won't let me down tomorrow.'

As he emerged from the dressing room, it was clear that Ryan Giggs knew what the result meant.

'It's a massive disappointment considering the run we have been on. We have produced so many great performances, but to not get full points tonight is really disappointing. It was a mixture of a lot of things: not enough composure in front of goal, their 'keeper producing great saves, sometimes not picking the right option, but the chances we got, we should be scoring.

'We were just concentrating on winning; the talk of it being four- or five-nil was never an issue within the team. We just had to win and that was the bottom line, to carry on the momentum, but we haven't managed to do that. Obviously the crowd gets anxious, but as players you have to ignore that and try to play your football. To be fair we created enough chances, but it just wasn't to be.

'No one saw this coming and that has probably been the story of the season. We have beaten the big teams, but if you look at the points we've dropped, City home and away, Blackburn, but against the likes of Chelsea, Arsenal, Liverpool we have had the results. It happened last year as well, so that is something we have to address for next season, because these are the games that win championships.

'We have a hard game against Tottenham on Monday and if we win that and the results go for us, you never know. But we have certainly made it very hard for ourselves now. At least the next game is coming quickly, it's tough, but one we are capable of winning if we show the form we have produced, not tonight, but in other games.

'We have to stand up and be counted as a team and as individuals; go away tonight and look at yourself and come back stronger. We have to react to tonight in a positive way and I am sure we will. You have to bounce back.'

Next day Chelsea won 2–0 at Bolton, putting the title within reach. Should United lose at Tottenham, it will be party time at The Bridge on Monday evening provided they beat Everton.

MONDAY 17 APRIL 2006

SCORER:
Rooney 8, 36
ATTENDANCE:
36,141

Barclays Premiership
Tottenham Hotspur 1   Manchester United 2

UNITED: VAN DER SAR, NEVILLE, FERDINAND, VIDIC, SILVESTRE, RONALDO (BROWN 89), O'SHEA, GIGGS, PARK, ROONEY, VAN NISTELROOY. SUBS NOT USED: HOWARD, EVRA, HEINZE, SAHA.

Chelsea's champagne stays on ice a little longer as United's show hits the road again with the twelfth away win of the season.

Sir Alex made two changes to the Sunderland line-up, bringing in Nemanja Vidic and Mikael Silvestre as Wes Brown and Patrice Evra dropped to the bench, but there was no starting place for Louis Saha, even though he had recovered from injury.

Spurs, looking for the win that might help them secure fourth place, were in a lively mood, with both Robbie Keane and Jermain Defoe going close early on. It stunned United into a response, which came with only eight minutes gone. A Tottenham corner was cleared. Van Nistelrooy found Ronaldo on the left. Using his speed, he created an opening, with Wayne Rooney sliding home his low cross from close range.

Ronaldo almost made it 2–0 after thirty-five minutes with a fierce header from a Gary Neville cross and, sixty seconds later, when Ji-sung Park forced fellow countryman Yong-Pyo Lee into a mistake, then found Rooney, he hammered home his sixteenth league goal of the season.

In the second half, Michael Carrick showed the class that has apparently been attracting interest from Sir Alex, and Jermaine Jenas made a fight of it by scoring from a Keane free kick in the fifty-third minute. United's defence stood firm and van Nistelrooy hit a post with a cracker three minutes from time.

The title race would stay alive for at least another twelve days, when United would face their rivals at Stamford Bridge, but when Chelsea beat Everton later in the day, it meant that they needed only one point from their remaining three games to be crowned champions. More to the point, with Liverpool winning their Easter Sunday game at Blackburn, the heat was still on to secure second place, according to Edwin van der Sar.

'It was very important for us to win today after seeing that result yesterday. We are still in the race for the title, but we know it is getting less and less likely we are going to do something after what happened at Old Trafford on Friday. It is sort of over and that is why it was important today to win and keep a six-point gap between us and Liverpool. The feeling in the camp is that Chelsea can't celebrate anything tonight, but we want to make it so that they can't celebrate after our game there, because we don't want to be part of that.'

Mikael Silvestre agreed: 'After Friday, the main thing was to come here and play our football, play like we have been playing for the last nine games and we did that. We have to keep going and grab as many points as we can, so all the games are going to be interesting until the end of the season.

'A win is excellent for us to get ready for the next game. We are going to have a lot of time to prepare for what is going to be a massive, massive game. We need to get a result over there, just for the pride, and we have beaten them already, so let's see what we can achieve at Stamford Bridge.

'Compared to the last two seasons where we haven't really finished the season with any conviction, this time everybody is fighting for a place in the team, fighting for the World Cup, so everybody has got his own goal and the best thing is that the team is winning.'

The long wait for the Chelsea showdown was brought about by the fact that the Londoners were on course for the Double. They were due to face Liverpool in the FA Cup semi-final a week before the Stamford Bridge clash, a game staged at Old Trafford. United should have played Middlesbrough that weekend, but the game was rescheduled because they too were involved in the cup with a semi-final against West Ham at Villa Park. What might have happened had the 'Boro game been played before United faced Chelsea is left to the imagination.

Both Chelsea and Middlesbrough were knocked out of the cup, and that may have given Sir Alex good reason to remain up beat on the eve of the big game.

'We won't change our approach. Every game we try to win and we will do that when we go down there. I don't think Chelsea will expect us to change, it is just a more interesting game than we have had for a few weeks.

'If we win tomorrow, it is still mathematically possible, but they are in the driving seat and I don't think there is any doubt about that. They can get a point in one of their next three games, so it is very difficult to say they are not going to win the league, but you never know.

'We are not giving up and will be trying to win, that's without question. What we want to do is play to our form, which has been good, and if we can get the result at least it ekes it out, makes it that little bit longer before they get their presentation. We can only achieve that by winning and see what happens from there.

'Chelsea's priority will be to try to get that presentation tomorrow and I don't know how they will go about it. They won't take anything other than a pragmatic view of it. Win the title, no matter how they are going to get it. They may set out with a system to get that point, they may go for broke, but they will want to get it over as quick as possible.'

Saturday 29 April 2006

Barclays Premiership
Chelsea 3   Manchester United 0

UNITED: VAN DER SAR, NEVILLE, FERDINAND, VIDIC, SILVESTRE, RONALDO (VAN NISTELROOY 65), O'SHEA, GIGGS (RICHARDSON 73), PARK, ROONEY (EVRA 82), SAHA. SUBS NOT USED: HOWARD, BROWN.

From bad to worse. Jose Mourinho's side led as early as the fourth minute and were crowned Premiership champions in front of their biggest rivals, but United were hit with a devastating blow when

Wayne Rooney was stretchered off. It happened eight minutes from the end, as he raced for the ball and was tackled by Paulo Ferreira, and even the home fans were silenced as they wondered about the implications, with the start of the World Cup just forty days away.

United started with Louis Saha coming in to replace Ruud van Nistelrooy, but it never was their day. William Gallas scored the opener with a close-range shot after Joe Cole's corner was knocked down by Didier Drogba; the Reds almost equalised twenty minutes later, when Rooney raced through, beat Petr Cech and then saw his shot roll wide, and John O'Shea headed over just before the break.

There was little to choose between the teams up to half time, with United making the brighter start after the break when Ronaldo went close; then Cole struck the killer blow hitting a rising shot beyond van der Sar on the hour. With United looking for a goal, they left gaps at the back and Carvalho made it 3–0, twelve minutes later. The chase was over: Chelsea were champions, but as they celebrated, with Rooney in the treatment room, United had other things on their mind.

As Wayne hobbled aboard the team coach on crutches, Sir Alex assessed the damage.

'We don't know how he is. He's had a heavy knock and we'll just have to wait and see when we get back to Manchester. At this stage we don't want to be making any opinions on it. He's in the right hands. Just as a matter of coincidence, our orthopaedic surgeon is down with us today; the club doctor, Mike Stone is there, and the physio, so we'll just wait and see.

'As for the game, I think the scoreline tells you that if you don't defend properly you are going to lose games like that. I don't think Edwin van der Sar had a save to make, whereas their 'keeper had three or four very good saves. The scoreline doesn't reflect the run of the game, but we let in some very soft goals and that is the only thing that disappoints me.'

As the Chelsea celebrations continued in the background, the manager added: 'You have to have the dignity to accept that another team has won the championship and there is no problem with us in that way. We have handled that well over the years. Our season has been galvanised by the form of recent times, but I am certain we are going to be right there among it next season.'

CHAPTER NINE

*Broken bones, broken hearts,
but Europe here we come!*

On the evening of Saturday 29 April, the club issued a statement on its official website. It read: 'Wayne Rooney has a fracture of the base of the fourth metatarsal on his right foot. He will be out for six weeks.'

The reaction was sensational, if not unexpected.

'England's World Cup dreams shattered,' screamed the back pages the following morning. It was the last thing Sir Alex wanted to read as United prepared for their final two games of the season. The journey from London was bad enough with photographers following every move and Wayne whisked to hospital as soon as the party arrived back in Manchester, but the pressure was now on to clinch second place.

Liverpool had beaten Aston Villa at Anfield in a game that kicked off after the match at Chelsea had ended. Goal difference was now the only thing separating the two, although United held a slight advantage because they had two games left. Liverpool's season would end at Fratton Park the following Sunday, when they played their one remaining fixture.

To say tension was high would be an understatement, with the manager determined to handle the Rooney situation his way, as well as preparing for what could prove a decisive game only two days after the Chelsea defeat. The re-arranged Middlesbrough fixture was possibly the last thing United wanted at such a time. A win might be enough to secure that Champions League qualifying place, but if

Steve McClaren's side was to do the double over the Reds, everything would hinge on the closing afternoon of the season.

MONDAY 1 MAY 2006

ATTENDANCE:
69,531

Barclays Premiership
Manchester United 0   Middlesbrough 0

UNITED: VAN DER SAR, NEVILLE, FERDINAND, BROWN, SILVESTRE, PARK (RONALDO 56), O'SHEA, GIGGS, EVRA (RICHARDSON 56), SAHA (ROSSI 81), VAN NISTELROOY. SUBS NOT USED: HOWARD, VIDIC.

Come back Wayne, United needs you! The message was clear on a frustrating night and oh, how they loved the scoreline on Merseyside, with United forced to go into the last game of the season needing a win. To make matters worse, Ruud van Nistelrooy missed a great chance to notch up his 151st goal under the easiest of circumstances when his penalty was saved in the sixty-fifth minute, and Boro proved once again that they truly are United's bogey team.

What proved the decisive moment came when Lee Cattermole handled a Giggs corner; United were rightly awarded the spot kick and Bradley Jones dived to his right to stop a poorly hit shot from the out-of-sorts Dutchman. United were a point ahead of Liverpool with Charlton coming to Old Trafford on Sunday and the Reds needing to equal or better the Merseysiders' result to finish second.

The fans were far from happy. As the teams were leaving the field, Gary Neville reacted brusquely to the critical comments of one supporter which led to Sir Alex later defending his skipper.

'We took some flak and Gary responded angrily in the face of the accusation we had not tried hard enough. Nobody can fault Gary in that area. He's passionate about this club and his reaction tells you how much he cares.'

There was a hint that all was not well though, when the manager was asked about the missed penalty from van Nistelrooy: 'The penalty was a bad miss. He's missed a few, but it was an important one today and I was hoping he would score it.'

However, it was the manager's reaction to the Rooney situation that made the headlines the next day.

Did Sir Alex expect him to go to Germany with England?

'What you have to do is make sure you don't build up the expectations of everyone, because that's what is happening at the moment. Sven-Goran Eriksson is saying he is taking him to Germany whether he is fit or not; now that's the kind of talk we don't want to hear.

'We are going to do our very best to get that boy to Germany, but we are going to monitor it and if he is not ready to go, then he won't be going. He can only go if he is fit. Players who perform on that stage are really honed to absolute 100 per cent fitness and it's really folly to suggest a boy can be out of the game for six or seven weeks and two weeks later is going to play in a quarter-final. We have got to calm people down.'

Did Sir Alex expect to be consulted every step of the way?

'We will be doing the consulting ourselves. We've got the right people here and we will make sure it's done properly.'

As for the player himself, he had no idea of how long it might take him to recover and was not building up any hopes, especially his own. Twenty-four hours after the Middlesbrough game, he appeared on MUTV saying: 'I'll be coming in every day for treatment and trying to give myself the best possible chance. I'm obviously devastated to have broken my foot at this moment in time. It really is horrible, but I'm in great hands at United and I know with the physio team I've got behind me here that they'll be able to give me the best possible chance. You've just got to get on with it and be positive. That's what I'm trying to do at the moment and I'll be trying to get myself fit as soon as possible.'

Wayne was in the spotlight the following evening when the club staged its first Players' Award Dinner at Old Trafford, one of the events marking the fiftieth anniversary of the Busby Babes' first championship success.

He joined a list of players that included Eric Cantona, Bryan Robson and Roy Keane, as he collected the Sir Matt Busby Player of the Year trophy after topping a poll of supporters' votes cast online at ManUtd.com and via text message. Other awards saw Cristiano Ronaldo pick up the Goal of the Season prize for his first strike in the 3–1 win at Portsmouth, while Giuseppe Rossi pipped Gerard Pique and Markus Neumayr in the poll to win the Denzil Haroun Reserve Team Player of the Year award. Ryan Giggs was named Players' Player of the Year by his team-mates, while Darron Gibson, who helped win the Barclays Premiership Reserve League title, was selected by the coaching staff as the Jimmy Murphy Young Player of the Year. The dinner raised over £35,000 for the Manchester United Foundation.

The following day focus was firmly on the weekend and Charlton Athletic. It was a crucial game, a fixture which would not only determine United's final finishing position but, more importantly, the manager's plans for the following season. Sir Alex was doing everything in his power to concentrate on securing second place, but the media would not deflect its attention away from Wayne Rooney.

When his pre-match conference began with a demand for a latest update on the forward's foot, the response was perhaps predictable.

'There's no update and I think the important thing for us as a club is to stop giving out statements. We have given the proper statement and the proper message about what we intend to do with the boy. As we have said, we will do our best to get him there and it's in our interests as well as England's to do that. There won't be any statements from the club again.'

Dealing with a broken metatarsal was nothing new to the United medical staff, and the manager was fully aware of the recovery time involved, having been robbed of key players in the past when they suffered similar setbacks.

'In our experience over the years, the likes of Gary Neville ended up having his pinned because he hadn't recovered properly. I think David Beckham made the mistake of joining up with England in Dubai. He would have been much fitter if he had stayed here, but he wanted to go with the England squad and I don't think he was fit enough to play in the World Cup.

'Roy Keane was ten or eleven weeks from getting the injury against Liverpool to leaving here and was going to play in the reserves on the Thursday before he went. That would have been his first game back. In the case of Wayne, with his last injury, it was fourteen weeks before he came back to play and we obviously don't want that kind of recovery. When you get an injury like that, there have to be doubts.'

And what about Charlton?

'This is a massive game now. But I always feel it's important to win the last home game of the season. We have to take second place and, hopefully, a good determined performance will get us there. It's typical United, we tend to do things the hard way, but I am sure we will get the right performance.'

Everything was ready for the curtain to come down on another season, but before it did, there would be more drama at Old Trafford and it began to unfold three hours before the closing game kicked off. Around noon, fans were surprised to see Ruud van Nistelrooy driving away from the ground. The routine ahead of home games is for players to leave their cars in a secure compound at Old Trafford before travelling by coach to the team hotel for an overnight stay and the normal pre-match preparations. The track-suited Dutchman had arrived at the ground by taxi, leaving in his own car minutes later and driving stony faced through ranks of bemused fans.

Two hours later, the club issued a statement confirming that the player had indeed left the stadium, adding: 'There is no further comment because we are concentrating on the game.'

SUNDAY 7 MAY 2006

Barclays Premiership
Manchester United 4   Charlton Athletic 0

UNITED: VAN DER SAR, NEVILLE (VIDIC 60), FERDINAND, BROWN, SILVESTRE, RONALDO, O'SHEA (SCHOLES 46), GIGGS, RICHARDSON, ROSSI, SAHA (SOLSKJAER 60). SUBS NOT USED: HOWARD, FLETCHER.

SCORERS:
Saha 19,
Ronaldo 23,
own goal 34,
Richardson 58

ATTENDANCE:
73,006

Exit Ruud van Nistelrooy, enter Giuseppe Rossi. The next generation of Manchester United got the chance to show what it can do, and Rossi rose to the occasion, going close to scoring several times in an impressive performance as the Reds tied up second spot. Goals from Saha, Ronaldo, and one from Jason Euell, who turned the ball into his own net under pressure, put United in the driving seat at the break before a super strike from Kieran Richardson tied things up.

Rossi's first Premiership start saw the nineteen-year-old add to an already impressive CV that has seen him top the thirty-goal mark for the title-winning reserves this season, with one of his goal attempts a spectacular diving header that really tested Charlton 'keeper Stephan Andersen.

As well as scoring, Richardson also rattled the underside of the bar with the ball coming out so quickly that it needed a television replay to confirm it had not crossed the line. The second half saw a surprise comeback for Paul Scholes, his first appearance since December, and in a carnival atmosphere Ole Gunnar Solskjaer and Nemanja Vidic also had a taste of the action as Louis Saha and Gary Neville stood down.

The season was over, but not the talking, and much of it was about van Nistelrooy.

Was there a problem?

'Well, there's been a couple of issues in training this week that concerned me in terms of the team spirit and I felt in such an important game we wanted everyone together. That's what we have done. We left Ruud out of it and we will discuss it with the directors and take it on from there. In management you have to make decisions and we made a decision today that was right for Manchester United. That's it.'

There were more pleasant surprises for the fans.

At the end of the game, when the players did their customary end-of-season lap of honour, Wayne Rooney was walking unaided. His foot was encased in a support, but no crutches.

'He is doing his treatment in the oxygen chamber twice a day and he's shown a great dedication to do that, because it's not the best thing to be sitting in, but he is doing it in the hope he will get to the World Cup.'

What did it mean to be runner-up?

'Just ask the players. They were all praying last night, because I told them if we didn't get second place they would have been back in on 15 July, but I thought they would rise to the occasion today. When the chips are down they don't let you down often.'

And the return of Paul Scholes?

'It was great to see the little lad back. Forty-five minutes of sheer joy and I don't think he lost the ball once. His imagination, his passing ability were all there and he enjoyed himself. He was delighted to be back. He's been training really well in the last three weeks and we got the all clear from the doctor for him to play, so there was no hesitation on my part.'

For Scholes himself there was a certain amount of relief to be playing again. Ordered to end his season in December and take a complete rest, it had been an ordeal.

'I still have a bit of blurred vision in my right eye, but I just want to get myself ready for next season. Obviously you are concerned when you are told it is serious and you have to rest, but in my own mind I was always confident I would be back playing again. The specialists wouldn't let me play on as it was, but now I feel I will be okay for next season.'

The problem was caused by a blocked vein in his eye and started just after Christmas when his sight mysteriously began to blur.

'I had a little bit of blurred vision before the Birmingham match. I told the medical staff after the match, then I went to see a specialist. He told me it was a quite serious condition and I had to take some time off. They assured me it would get better but they didn't know whether it would be three months, six months or whatever. I was just ordered to rest.'

Paul was not the only one looking forward to the 2006–07 season.

There was an atmosphere of expectancy throughout the squad as they looked back on what had been an eventful season. Ryan Giggs saw it as: 'A tale of two halves. Before Christmas we weren't playing well, maybe confidence was a little bit low and we had some disappointing results, then afterwards we played really well. We went on a great run of Premiership games and, of course, we won the League Cup as well.

'When you start off the season, you want to go for as many trophies as you can. The Champions League and the league are the main ones, but to win a trophy is great for everyone involved and next year we will be looking to improve.

'One thing we need to address is our home form. I don't know what it is, but that seems to have been the case for the last couple of years. When we were dominating the Premiership, Old Trafford was a fortress and teams were coming here fearing the worst, but we have had some disappointing home games for whatever reason. If we are going to be challenging for the Premiership next year, that is something we need to address and improve on.

'It's exciting to see the players who are at the club now and the age of those players. We have a really young squad at the moment and hopefully they will all grow up together and become a great team. I am excited to see young talent coming through like it is; that is part of the history of United and it will never change.'

Gerard Pique and Giuseppe Rossi have shown that they can do it?

'The ability is undoubtedly there. The thing for them now is taking that step from the reserves into the first team, which so many players do with ease, but some don't. I am sure the ability and the temperament is there for the two of them and Man United has a great history of bringing young players through and, hopefully, next season we will see a lot more of Pique and Rossi, because they are great talents.

'If you are a good player you are going to get in the team or the squad. If you are doing the right things in the youth team and the reserves, the manager is going to see that. The thing about this club, and the manager we have got, is that he is never afraid to put young players into the first team and he has always had the philosophy that if you are good enough, then you are old enough.

'I think it is great for young players to see that and to continue seeing young players coming through into the first team. There was the group of us when I was that age, recently there's been Fletch and Sheasy, Kieran and Phil Bardsley. It's great.

'The manager has brought down the age of the team, apart from the likes of me and Scholesy and Nev. We are the more experienced older players now, but generally the squad is a young one and you just hope that all the ability that's there can be nurtured into a great team.'

What about the challenge of Chelsea?

'Even though they weren't playing well at the start of the season they were getting results and we weren't, and maybe we would have done in the past. That is what we have got to try to sort out: to get results when we have not played well.

'Liverpool at home, for example. We didn't play well, Liverpool had a few chances, but we ended up winning the game in the last minute. That's what it's all about: digging in and winning those scruffy games. We know we are capable of playing brilliant football and scoring three or four goals, but it is those one-nil results or those difficult away games where it is snatch and grab, winning games at the death, which matter.

'Maybe it is just that killer punch; even in the games where we have played well, we haven't killed teams off like we used to. That's something we need to work on. You have to have confidence and learn from games like Sunderland; perhaps we need to be a bit more patient ... don't just go out in the first half and feel that you need to score two or three goals.

'Next season we hope to win the Premiership. We went on a great run at the end of the season and just hope we can improve on where we faltered, the stupid points we have given away in certain games. The ability is undoubtedly there; we have done great against the big teams. Maybe it's just the lack of concentration at certain points where we have come up against teams we expect to beat and you find yourself stuck because you haven't gone out and got the three points.

'You have to give credit to Chelsea because they are so consistent. That is what we will be looking for next season. I feel we have got the best team but, consistency wise, Chelsea are a little bit better than us at the moment.'

Fighting talk from the club's longest serving player, and a view supported by skipper Gary Neville as he looked back on a campaign marred by injuries to experienced players – himself included.

'I had two or three months out, missed a lot of Man United games, missed a few England games. In that period it was a difficult time for the club. We took a lot of criticism, lost a couple of games in Europe and it wasn't just me who had got injured around that time there were a few more … Gabriel Heinze, and Keaney was injured for a period, Giggsy missed a few, Wes Brown, and we sort of just struggled to get any continuation of selection and consistency at the start of the season which ultimately set us back. Really, we recovered well and finished the season strongly because we finally got that consistency and fitness throughout the team.'

Did he share the opinion that the young talent at the club is good enough to predict a new period of success is close at hand?

'Definitely, but I don't think the void is with the young players. People can point to the young players, but sometimes I think that maybe a little more experience, certainly in the central midfield area is what we need. We lost Scholesy to his problem, Quinton Fortune, Roy Keane, Alan Smith as well as Philip Neville and Nicky Butt. We have lost all those players through really bad injuries or them leaving the club and there is so much experience there. We are probably lacking that bit of experience in the central midfield area, but I am sure that will be sorted out by the manager.

'The young players are fine – Rio, Rooney, Ronaldo, Wes. These types of players, they are fantastic and they are going to get better and better. They'll mature and show more composure, and hopefully there can be a bit more of a balance and we can keep our players fit. This season really, players leaving and losing others through injuries, has had a massive effect on us, especially going out of Europe.

'That was a huge blow for us. People talked about us losing to Benfica in Lisbon and that was where we got knocked out, but Benfica were a good team and went on to prove it since by beating Liverpool. They are a good side, but we didn't lose it against Benfica, we lost it at home against Lille, against Villarreal, away against Lille.

'You can't point to excuses, but we were really decimated by injuries. Roy was missing, I was missing, Gabriel Heinze was missing, Ryan did his cheekbone and we were without some really big players. Key players. The ones who were experienced and who would have brought a little bit of authority into the games.

'Lille were a poor team and to get one point out of Lille was where we lost it. That's where we got knocked out of Europe and it was just because of being decimated with injuries, and through that we lost confidence and hit poor form around that time.'

John O'Shea was another who looked forward to a renewed European challenge after the disappointment of the pre-Christmas exit.

'That was an absolute bombshell. It was amazing to think that if we had scored just one more goal in any of the games it would have been enough to get us through. Especially for the way we play, our style of football. To not score enough goals was a blow. It was nowhere near what we usually score and ultimately that cost us. We had too many draws, not enough goals and for the first time in ten or eleven seasons we were out before the knockout phase.

'Probably every player can remember a moment during one of the games when he might have scored and that would have been enough. In games like Villarreal at home and even when we played them away, we had ten men for the last half hour but before that had chances to score. Then you look at Benfica away and we had chances there to kill them off but it didn't happen.'

John, Ryan and Gary were all in the squad for the game which saw United beat Celtic 1–0 and signalled the start of the summer break. On Tuesday 9 May, Roy Keane returned to Old Trafford for his testimonial. It was a game granted by the club when he had left in November and, according to the former captain, was an opportunity to draw a line under his days with United. Close to a capacity crowd saw Keane play the first half for Celtic, the second for United and afterwards he spoke about his decision to walk away from Old Trafford after more than twelve years.

'It was bad timing in the sense I was injured, it was November and I couldn't sign for another club until January, but I agreed with the manager. It had come to an end. There is never a nice way to leave a club, especially one like United when I had been there for so long, but we both knew it was for the best and there is no doubt in my mind that is true. It was all very amicable and I certainly do not lose any sleep about it. I have met the manager on one or two occasions since and there is no problem.'

Missing from the United squad was van Nistelrooy, and Roy Keane was diplomatic when asked to comment about the Dutchman's absence.

'There are two sides to every story. Maybe one day we will find out what happened, but I don't know. I always got on quite well with Ruud. He is still under contract to United and I wish him well.'

For Sir Alex the close season was a time to plan ahead. The Premiership's longest-serving and most successful manager ended the campaign convinced he was on the verge of bringing more glory to Old Trafford. He is in the process of building a young team and claims the players currently with the club are the best he has ever had and, because of that, he can confidently predict a bright future.

'Oh yes. It is always difficult, but being here nineteen years – twenty in November – probably gives me the best view of the standards we have had. Therefore, I take it seriously when people say "It's not like the great days, and the great players we brought through like Giggs and all the others, Beckham, Scholes, Butt, the Nevilles."

'That was a one-off miracle. It wasn't a miracle in one sense, because of the work that we put into it. We worked our socks off. We were working harder than any other club in the country at scouting, trialling, making decisions, me going to see parents everywhere. I drove up to the Northeast one night, snow all the way there, snow all the way back, got done for speeding in Halifax coming back at two in the morning and things like that. We worked harder than anyone to get players signed.

'We were speaking to parents, having them over here and taking them to dinner on Friday nights. I was never out of that bloody Wendover Hotel. We used to put the parents in there and I would go for dinner with them on Friday nights getting them right for the weekend, then down to London and I will always remember bringing John Terry up here for dinner, him and his parents when he was only thirteen years old. That is how David Beckham came in. We made David our mascot at West Ham once, but his mother used to say "he'll never grow", and of course when he got to sixteen he sprouted like nothing on earth.

'Our scouting is always judged because of those players from 1996, but that is not quite fair because it was a one-off, but what we have done is, over the years, we have developed a consistent stream of young players who have done well in the game, not necessarily always playing for Man United.

'In the present squad you've got John O'Shea, Wes Brown, Darren Fletcher, Pique, Rossi. We've got the two Jones boys, one's in Holland and doing very well, scoring six goals in eight games. Chris Eagles is playing at Watford, the young boy Lee Martin is doing fantastic at Antwerp. We are a very vibrant club in terms of getting young players and the squad, quite rightly, is as good as we have had.

'When you are manager of this club for a long time, I always remember Jock Stein saying, "Remember one thing. You fall in love with players and we all do, you maybe have one particular favourite, or something like that, but you can't let the favouritism detract from you doing your job. You have favourites. We all have favourites, we have great players and you do tend to fall in love with them."

'But when you have a group of players for a long time, like we had in the 1999 side, and it built up to that great success, then they get old and it changes. Denis Irwin got old, Roy Keane got old, Ronny Johnsen got old and got some injuries, Peter Schmeichel retired, Andy Cole got into his thirties and we got a great offer for him from

Blackburn and I thought it was right to take it. Teddy got old, but he is still playing! He got a sensational, fantastic offer from Tottenham and I said to him, "Take it, you can't turn it down." So you have to then look ahead to see where you can be in two or three years' time. That is the hard part at this club, because as you do that you have still got to be successful.

'The hard thing is to change, to evolve the team and still be successful, while also having an eye for the future. That is why winning the Carling Cup can be important. Cristiano and Wayne are only kids, but they are leaders too. Those two are leaders. Absolutely. You take my word for it, Cristiano Ronaldo is a leader, an absolute leader. He is a magnificent personality: intelligent, powerful, strong, courageous. He is a leader: him and Rooney are the leaders of the new team.'

How long will the fans have to wait before United win the Premiership again?

'I hope it is next year [2006–07]. I think it could be next year. I don't see why not. Our consistency since we got knocked out against Benfica has been good, although we have done it under unusual circumstances. We lost Paul Scholes and had to do with makeshift midfields, but what has galvanised it is the performances of Rooney, Ronaldo, Saha, Ji-sung Park and van Nistelrooy; with forwards like that, it gives you a chance of winning games.

'That is paramount to what has been happening in the last few months and with bringing in Vidic and Evra, it gives me good alternatives at the back now. As we know, Wes does get injuries and that, unfortunately, is just the make-up of the lad. Vidic is getting better with every kick of the ball.

'Gabriel Heinze will be fit again for the start of the new season, he is back now. We will definitely be adding. I have spoken to the Glazer family and they have given me the go-ahead to go for who I want, so in that respect we are scouting very strongly, so that is important. We are also doing it in a different way, because the competition is greater and we are keeping our cards close to our chest now trying to prevent any knowledge getting out and it is amazing the things we are doing now to keep that quiet.'

Who else will be challenging in the new season?

'You have to think that Chelsea's buying power is going to keep them up there as a threat to everyone, but you can see an improvement in us and Arsenal without question. Moving to a new stadium will be a great motivation for Arsenal, a lift for the players and for the fans, but whether they can fill it consistently I am not so sure. They will fill it in the early part, but it depends what they are charging, of course, because the London prices are ridiculous.

'You will see an improvement in Tottenham, too. They have got the bit between their teeth in terms of buying. All of a sudden they just decide to go and buy players all over the place and it has got them into a better position than they have been in for years. You would also expect Liverpool to be buying, because a new owner might just put a bit of money in so it could turn out to be the most competitive league of all time.'

And Manchester United will be going all out to win it.